WJEC EDUQAS GCSE STUDENT BOOK

English Language

Assessment preparation for Component 1 and Component 2

Michelle Doran

Natalie Simpson

Julie Swain

Consultant:
Barry Childs

OXFORD
UNIVERSITY PRESS

OXFORD
UNIVERSITY PRESS

Great Clarendon Street, Oxford, OX2 6DP, United Kingdom

Oxford University Press is a department of the University of Oxford. It furthers the University's objective of excellence in research, scholarship, and education by publishing worldwide. Oxford is a registered trade mark of Oxford University Press in the UK and in certain other countries

British Library Cataloguing in Publication Data

Data available

ISBN 978-019-833283-1

10 9 8 7 6 5 4

Printed in China by Golden Cup

Acknowledgements

The authors and publisher are grateful for permission to reprint extracts from the following copyright material:

Douglas Adams: *The Restaurant at the End of the Universe* (Pan Books, 1980), copyright © Douglas Adams 1980, reprinted by permission of Ed Victor Ltd for the Estate of Douglas Adams.

David Almond: *The Fire Eaters* (Hodder Children's Books, 2013), copyright © David Almond 2003, reprinted by permission of the publishers, an imprint of Hachette Children's Books, Carmelite House, 50 Victoria Embankment, London EC4Y 0DZ.

Margaret Atwood: 'Two stories about Emma' in *Bluebeard's Egg and Other Stories* (Cape, 1987), copyright © O W Toad 1983, reprinted by permission of and Curtis Brown Group Ltd, London on behalf of O W Toad Ltd.

Tom Clancy: *The Hunt for Red October* (HarperCollins, 2010), copyright © Tom Clancy 1985, reprinted by permission of HarperCollins Publishers Ltd.

Hans Fallada translated by Michael Hoffman: *Alone in Berlin* (Penguin Classics, 2009), first published as Jeder stirbt für sich allein, 1947, translation first published by Melville House Publishing, 2009, copyright © Aufbau-Verlagsgruppe GmbH, Berlin 1994, translation copyright © Michael Hoffmann 2009, reprinted by permission of Penguin Books Ltd.

Jane Fryer: 'Wimp who walks on water...', *Daily Mail*, 9 July 2012, copyright © 2012, reprinted by permission of Solo Syndication/ Mail Online

Mick Gradwell: 'The hidden world of modern day slave trade' by, *Lancashire Evening Post*, 2 Oct 2014, reprinted by permission of the author and the Lancashire Evening Post, www.lep.co.uk

Graham Greene: *Travels with My Aunt* (Vintage, 1999), copyright © Graham Greene 1969, reprinted by permission of David Higham Associates.

Elizabeth Laird: *Red Sky in the Morning* (Macmillan Children's Books, 2001), copyright © Elizabeth Laird 1988, reprinted by permission of the publishers.

Mary Lawson: *Crow Lake* (Chatto & Windus, 2002), reprinted by permission of The Random House Group Ltd.

Michael Morpurgo: *Twist of Gold* (Egmont 2011), copyright © Michael Morpurgo 1993, reprinted by permission of David Higham Associates.

Alice Munro: 'Dance of the Happy Shades' in *Dance of the Happy Shades: and other stories* (Vintage, 2000), reprinted by permission of The Random House Group Ltd.

David Nicholls: *One Day* (Hodder & Stoughton, 2009), copyright © David Nicholls 2009, reprinted by permission of Hodder & Stoughton Ltd.

Robin Pagnamenta: 'The cotton in your clothes may be made by girls aged 11, paid £6 a month', *The Times*, 15 Nov 2014, copyright © Robin Pagnamenta/News UK and Ireland Ltd 2014, reprinted by permission of News Syndication.

Owen Sheers: *Resistance* (Faber, 2011), copyright © Owen Sheers 2007, reprinted by permission of Faber & Faber Ltd.

Anita Shreve: *Light on Snow* (Abacus, 2004), copyright © Anita Shreve 2004, reprinted by permission of Little, Brown Book Group Ltd.

Robert Swindells: *Brother in the Land* (Puffin, 2000), copyright © Robert Swindells 1984, reprinted by permission of Oxford University Press.

Marcel Theroux: *The Paperchase* (Abacus, 2001), reprinted by permission of Aitken Alexander Associates.

Paul Mark Tag: 'The Long Walk Home', copyright © Paul Mark Tag, from storybytes.com, reprinted by permission of the author.

H G Wells: 'The Stolen Body', first published in *The Strand* in 1898, from *The Complete Short Story Omnibus* (Victor Gollancz, 2011), reprinted by permission of A P Watt at United Agents on behalf of The Literary Executors of the Estate of H G Wells.

Carlos Luis Zafón translated by Lucia Graves: *Shadow of the Wind* (Phoenix, 2004), copyright © Carlos Luis Zafón 2001, translation copyright © Lucia Graves 2004, reprinted by permission of The Orion Publishing Group.

and to the following for their permission to reprint from copyright material:

The Association of Graduate Careers Advisory Services (AGCAS) and Graduate Prospects for extract from Police Officer job description from www.prospects.ac.uk, copyright © AGCAS/ Graduate Prospects 2015.

Beddgelert Tourism Association for extract about Gelert from www.beddgelerttourism.com

Guardian News and Media Ltd for 'The Stig and I: My Top Gear adventure' by Tim Dowling, the guardian.com 4 Aug 2014, copyright © Guardian News & Media Ltd 2014; 'Ofcom: six-year-olds understand digital technology better than adults' by Juliette Garside, theguardian.com, 7 Aug 2014, copyright © Guardian News & Media Ltd 2014; 'Artist creates space for public to hear music' by Alex Needham, theguardian.com, 12 Sept 2014, copyright © Guardian News & Media Ltd 2014; and 'A Mother shakes her child in public - do you step in?' by Carla Power, the guardian.com, 8 Aug 2014, copyright © Guardian News & Media Ltd 2014.

ESI Media/The Independent (www.independent.co.uk) for 'DIY: SOS: The Big Build', BBC1 - TV Review by Ellen Jones, *The Independent*, 13 May 2014, copyright © The Independent 2014; 'Commuters of Britain: unite against the aural tyranny!' by Simon Kelner, *The Independent*, 6 Aug 2014, copyright © The Independent 2014; and 'Generatio text gets more screen time than sleep' by Joe Mayes, *The Independent*, 7 Aug 2014, copyright © The Independent 2014.

Reader Offers Ltd for extract from a Hurtigruten Voyage advert, 'Discover the Northern Lights'.

Telegraph Media Group for 'Borrow my dog; the website for part-time dog lovers' by Tom Cox, *The Telegraph*, 1 Oct 2014, copyright © Telegraph Media Group Ltd 2014; and 'Missing Australian Woman safe after 17 days in the bush' by Leon Siciliano, *The Telegraph*, 9 Oct 2014, copyright © Telegraph Media Group Ltd 2014.

Although we have made every effort to trace and contact all copyright holders before publication this has not been possible in all cases. If notified, the publisher will rectify any errors or omissions at the earliest opportunity.

The authors and publisher would like to thank the following for permissions to use their photographs:

Cover image: © Mira/Alamy; **p10–11**: Image by Catherine MacBride/Getty Images; **p12**: Dinga/Shutterstock; **p13**: Moviestore/REX; **p15**: Igor Zh./Shutterstock; **p16–17**: Dariusz Kantorski/Shutterstock; **p18–19**: Evgheni Manciu/Shutterstock; **p20**: littleny/Shutterstock; **p23**: hxdyl/Shutterstock; **p24–25**: THPStock/Shutterstock; **p26–27**: Erwin Niemand/Shutterstock; **p28**: © AF archive/Alamy; **p29**: charles taylor/Shutterstock; **p30–31**: Vadim Sadovski/Shutterstock; **p33**: Marafona/Shutterstock; **p34**: Stacey Newman/Shutterstock; **p36–37**: © All Canada Photos/Alamy; **p38**: © Michael Matthews - Police Images/Alamy; **p39**: Elena Elisseeva/Shutterstock; **p40**: © Erik Isakson/Tetra Images/Corbis; **p42**: 2nix Studio/Shutterstock; **p43**: Jaromir Chalabala/Shutterstock; **p46–47**: © allotment boy 1/Alamy; **p48**: © dpa picture alliance/Alamy; **p50–51**: Ksenia Ragozina/Shutterstock; **p51**: Samuel Burt/iStockphoto; **p54–55**: Oleksii Pyltsyn/Shutterstock; **p56**: Andrea Obzerova/iStockphoto; **p57**: EpicStockMedia/Shutterstock; **p58**: Cody Wheeler/Shutterstock; **p59**: © Steve Hamblin/Alamy; **p60**: (t) ATIC12/iStockphoto, (b) Ollyy/Shutterstock; **p61**: R.Iegosyn/Shutterstock; **p62**: Stephen Coburn/Shutterstock; **p63**: (t) 06photo/Shutterstock, (b) Photobac/Shutterstock; **p65**: Sadeugra/iStockphoto; **p66–67**: Dragon Images/Shutterstock; **p68–69**: pjhpix/Shutterstock; **p70**: © Michael Nolan/Robert Harding World Imagery/Corbis; **p70–71**: Koonyongyut/iStockphoto; **p72**: (t) phugunfire/Shutterstock, (b) defpicture/Shutterstock; **p72–73**: wang song/Shutterstock; **p74**: © Hulton-Deutsch Collection/CORBIS; **p75**: © Bettmann/CORBIS; **p76**: © abstract images/Alamy; **p77**: (m) © Simon Whaley/Alamy, (r) Paul J Martin/Shutterstock; **p79**: © Simon Whaley/Alamy; **p80**: (t) Bakhur Nick/Shutterstock, (b) © Terry Scott/Demotix/Corbis; **p81**: Mary Evans/Classic Stock/Sipley; **p82–83**: With kind permission from Predator Experience, predatorexperience.co.uk; **p83**: © Hal Beral/Corbis; **p84**: Ammit Jack/Shutterstock; **p85**: (t) Rock and Wasp/Shutterstock, (b) Lobstrosity/Shutterstock; **p86**: moreimages/Shutterstock; **p87**: (background) Quka/Shutterstock, (b) © Barry Diomede/Alamy; **p88**: (t) © Edward Herdwick/Alamy, (b) © Edward Herdwick/Alamy; **p89**: Kevin Eaves/Shutterstock; **p90–91**: michaket/Shutterstock; **p91**: (t) © Koen van Weel/epa/Corbis, (b) © culture-images GmbH/Alamy; **p92**: © Mark Bourdillon/Alamy; **p93**: © Mary Evans Picture Library/Alamy; **p94**: Courtesy of Wolfgang Tillmans; **p95**: Eugenio Marongiu/Shutterstock; **p96**: (t) Monkey Business Images/Shutterstock, (b) JM-Design/Shutterstock; **p98–99**: © GL Archive/Alamy; **p98**: © GL Archive/Alamy; **p101**: (t) BBC Photo Library, (b) Isara Kaenla/Shutterstock; **p103**: © adrian arbib/Alamy; **p104**: (tr) © Friedrich Stark/Alamy (bl) © World History Archive/Alamy; **p107**: © Neil Cooper/Alamy; **p108**: Ljupco Smokovski/Shutterstock; **p109**: (t) Jake Walters/Contour by Getty Images, (b) © INTERFOTO/Alamy; **p110**: (t) © Michael Dalder/Reuters/Corbis, (b) © The Print Collector/Alamy; **p111**: Milles Studio/Shutterstock; **p112**: Jaromir Chalabala/Shutterstock; **p113**: (t) © Richard Morrell/Corbis, (b) Mary Evans Picture Library/GROSVENOR PRINTS; **p114**: fasphotographic/Shutterstock; **p115**: (t) pcruciatti/Shutterstock, (b) © Wolverhampton City Council - Arts and Heritage/Alamy; **p117**: (t) Suzanne Tucker/Shutterstock, (b) Hung Chung Chih/Shutterstock; **p118**: Peshkova/Shutterstock; **p119**: SpeedKingz/Shutterstock; **p120**: Rawpixel/Shutterstock; **p123**: Monkey Business Images/Shutterstock; **p124–125**: Hitdelight/Shutterstock; **p126**: MarkauMark/Shutterstock; **p126–127**: Bukhavets Mikhail/Shutterstock; **p127**: l i g h t p o e t/Shutterstock; **p128–129**: Racheal Grazias/Shutterstock; **p130–131**: joyfull/Shutterstock; **p132**: (l) Tom Gowanloc Shutterstock, (r) Stephen Rees/Shutterstock; **p133**: (t) © redsnapper/Alamy, (b) Catherine Lane/iStockphoto; **p135**: © keith morris/Alamy; **p136–137**: Joseph Sohm/Shutterstock; **p138**: Monkey Business Images/Shutterstock; **p140**: mertcan/Shutterstock; **p141**: Tyler Olson/Shutterstock; **p142**: (t) haveseen/Shutterstock, (b) Goran Djukanovic/Shutterstock; **p143**: © Studio Works/Alamy; **p144**: Mark Sayer/Shutterstock; **p145**: Madrugada Verde/Shutterstock; **p146**: c.20thC.Fox/Everett/REX; **p147**: © Pictorial Press Ltd/Alamy; **p148**: © CORBIS; **p149**: © WENN UK/Alamy; **p150**: Alina Solovyova-Vincent/iStockphoto; **p151**: Syda Productions/Shutterstock; **p152**: Pressmaster/Shutterstock; **p152–153**: Lonely/Shutterstock; **p154**: Niloo/Shutterstock; **p155**: Warren Goldswain/Shutterstock; **p156**: Fer Gregory/Shutterstock; **p157**: Kzenon/Shutterstock; **p158–159**: hecke61/Shutterstock; **p160**: r.nagy/Shutterstock; **p162**: bikeriderlondon/Shutterstock; **p163**: isaravut/Shutterstock; **p166–167**: Pakhnyushchy/Shutterstock; **p173**: (l) Majority World/UIG via Getty Images; (r) © Kennet Havgaard/Aurora Photos/Corbis; **p175**: ©Mary Evans/Glasshouse Images

Designed and produced by Kamae Design.

CONTENTS

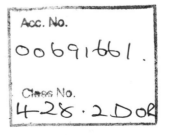
3

WJEC Eduqas GCSE English Language specification overview

The exam papers

The grade you receive at the end of your WJEC Eduqas GCSE English Language course is entirely based on your performance in two exam papers. The following provides a summary of these two exam papers:

Exam paper	Reading and Writing questions and marks	Assessment Objectives	Timing	Marks (and % of GCSE)
Component 1: 20th Century Literature **Reading and Creative Prose Writing**	**Section A: Reading** Exam text: • Extract from one unseen 20th-century literature prose text (about 60–100 lines) Exam questions and marks: • Five reading questions (40 marks in total)	Reading: • AO1 • AO2 • AO4	1 hour 45 minutes	Reading: 40 marks (20% of GCSE) Writing: 40 marks (20% of GCSE) Component 1 total: 80 marks (40% of GCSE)
	Section B: Writing Creative prose writing Exam questions and marks: • Choice of four titles – students respond to one task (24 marks for communication and organization; 16 marks for technical accuracy)	Writing: • AO5 • AO6		
Component 2: 19th and 21st Century Non-Fiction **Reading and Transactional/ Persuasive Writing**	**Section A: Reading** Exam texts: • Two unseen non-fiction texts (about 900–1200 words in total), one from the 19th century and the other from the 21st century Exam questions and marks: • Six reading questions (40 marks in total)	Reading: • AO1 • AO2 • AO3 • AO4	2 hours	Reading: 40 marks (30% of GCSE) Writing: 40 marks (30% of GCSE) Component 2 total: 80 marks (60% of GCSE)
	Section B: Writing Transactional/persuasive writing Exam question and marks: • Two compulsory tasks (20 marks for each task – 12 for communication and organization and 8 for technical accuracy)	Writing: • AO5 • AO6		

What will you be studying and learning?

Reading

Across the two GCSE English Language components, you will be studying the following:

- Critical reading and comprehension
- Summary and synthesis
- Evaluation of a writer's choice of vocabulary, form, grammatical and structural features
- Comparing texts

Writing

Across the two GCSE English Language components, you will be studying the following:

- Producing clear and coherent texts
- Writing for impact

Component 1 gives you opportunities for writing to describe and narrate, and imaginative and creative use of language. Your response should be narrative or recount.

Component 2, across the two tasks, gives you the opportunity to write for a range of audiences and purposes, adapting style to form and to real-life contexts in, for example, letters, articles, reviews, speeches, etc.

Spoken Language

As well as preparing for the two GCSE English Language exams, your course also includes Spoken Language assessment. This is **not** an exam. Instead you will be completing one formal presentation or speech where you will be:

- Presenting information and ideas
- Responding to spoken language
- Expressing ideas using Standard English

Spoken Language assesses AO7, AO8 and AO9. Your achievement in Spoken Language will be reported, but it will not form part of your final GCSE English Language qualification mark and grade.

A note on spelling

Certain words, for example 'synthesize' and 'organize', have been spelt with 'ize' throughout this book. It is equally acceptable to spell these words with 'ise'.

Introduction to this book

How this book will help you

Develop your reading and writing skills

This structure of this book reflects the structure of the two exam papers you will be taking, known as Component 1 and Component 2. Both exams have a Reading section followed by a Writing section. This book takes you through the types of questions you may be asked in both sections and provides guidance and activities to help you practise the skills that will be tested in the exams. The book also includes sample student answers, at different levels, and concludes with full sample exam papers.

Explore the types of texts that you will face in the exams

In your English Language exams, you will have to respond to a number of unseen texts. This book includes a range of texts and text types to help prepare you for the types of unseen texts that you will face in your exams. You will also explore connections between texts. The unseen texts in your exam papers will be of different types (fiction and non-fiction), from different historical periods (from the 19th, 20th and 21st centuries) and will, in some instances, be connected.

Become familiar with the Assessment Objectives

Assessment Objectives are the skills that underpin all qualifications. Your GCSE English Language exam papers are testing six Assessment Objectives (see below and page 4). This book develops your reading and writing skills, in the context of both the exam papers and these Assessment Objectives.

The Assessment Objectives

AO1	• Identify and interpret explicit and implicit information and ideas. • Select and synthesize evidence from different texts.
AO2	Explain, comment on and analyse how writers use language and structure to achieve effects and influence readers, using relevant subject terminology to support their views.
AO3	Compare writers' ideas and perspectives, as well as how these are conveyed, across two or more texts.
AO4	Evaluate texts critically and support this with appropriate textual references.
AO5	• Communicate clearly, effectively and imaginatively, selecting and adapting tone, style and register for different forms, purposes and audiences. • Organize information and ideas, using structural and grammatical features to support coherence and cohesion of texts.
AO6	Use a range of vocabulary and sentence structures for clarity, purpose and effect, with accurate spelling and punctuation.
AO7	Demonstrate presentation skills in a formal setting.
AO8	Listen and respond appropriately to spoken language, including to questions and feedback on presentations.
AO9	Use spoken Standard English effectively in speeches and presentations.

How is the book structured?

Component 1 and Component 2

This book is divided into two main sections covering Component 1 (Reading and Writing) and Component 2 (Reading followed by Writing). Within each of the Reading and Writing sections, the main skills are drawn out and these form the basis of the main teaching and learning throughout the book.

Each Reading and Writing section opens by:

- explaining where the section fits in terms of the exam Components
- summarizing the main skills
- outlining the relevant Assessment Objectives, together with AO strand and element references (as detailed in the WJEC Eduqas sample assessment materials)
- providing initial activities.

Technical accuracy accounts for 20% of the marks in your GCSE English Language qualification. Support for this is provided in the context of the writing tasks throughout the book.

The book concludes with sample exam papers, to enable you and your teacher to see how much progress you have made, and to provide a mock exam opportunity.

What are the main features within this book?

Activities

To develop your reading responses to the wide range of texts included in this book, as well as developing your writing skills, you will find many varied activities. These activities will help develop and improve your exam-response skills.

Activity 1

Tips, Key terms and glossed words

These features help support your understanding of key terms, concepts and more difficult words within a source text. These therefore enable you to concentrate fully on developing your reading and writing skills.

Tip

Key terms

Progress check

Throughout the book, you will find regular formative assessments in the form of 'Progress checks'. Through peer and self-assessment, these enable you to assess your learning and establish next steps and targets.

Progress check

Further GCSE English Language and GCSE English Literature resources

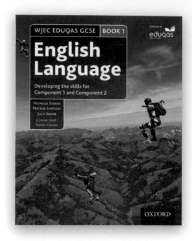

WJEC Eduqas GCSE English Language Student Book 1: Developing the skills for Component 1 and Component 2

Student Book 1 develops vital reading and writing skills in engaging thematic contexts, while also focusing on the Assessment Objectives linked to the requirements of the exams. This book is ideal for the start of the GCSE course and features:

- development of in-depth reading and writing skills in thematic contexts
- differentiated support and stretch activities, with an embedded focus on technical accuracy
- an Assessment Objective focus linked to the requirements of the exams
- opportunities for peer and self-assessment
- regular formative and summative assessments, including sample exam papers.

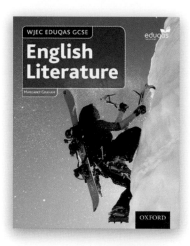

WJEC Eduqas GCSE English Literature Student Book

This Student Book provides in-depth skills development for the English Literature specification, including:

- comprehensive coverage and practice of the poetry anthology and unseen poetry requirements
- advice and activities to support Shakespeare, the 19th-century novel and modern prose and drama
- sample student responses at different levels and sample exam-style tasks to help prepare you for the exam paper questions
- 'Stretch' and 'Support' features to ensure all students make progress.

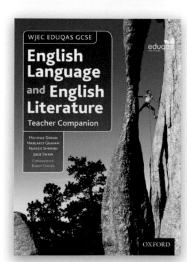

WJEC Eduqas GCSE English Language and English Literature Teacher Companion

The Teacher Companion provides holistic support for teachers to help them plan and deliver their GCSE programme, including:

- specification insight and planning guidance to aid planning and delivery of the specifications
- teaching tips and guidance for effective lesson delivery to all students of the material in Student Book 1, with additional support for differentiation and personalization
- extensive exam preparation guidance and planning, with links to English Language Student Book 2 and English Literature Student Book
- guidance and support for delivering Spoken Language assessments
- links to, and guidance on, the additional resources on Kerboodle.

WJEC Eduqas GCSE English Language and English Literature Kerboodle: Resources and Assessment

What is Kerboodle?

Kerboodle is a brand new online subscription-based platform provided by Oxford University Press.

Kerboodle: Resources and Assessment

This WJEC Eduqas GCSE English Language and English Literature Kerboodle: Resources and Assessment provides comprehensive support and resources to enable English departments and individual teachers to plan their GCSE courses and deliver effective, personalized lessons that prepare students for the requirements of the exams. Resources include:

- Teaching and learning materials, linked to the corresponding Student Books and Teacher Companion, including:
  - differentiation, personalization and peer/self-assessment worksheets and teaching resources
  - a bank of assignable spelling, punctuation and grammar interactive activities to improve technical accuracy
- Assessment resources, including:
  - marked sample answers to the Student Book 1 and Student Book 2 assessments, with mark schemes
  - editable versions of the end-of-chapter Student Book assessments and sample exam papers
- Professional development materials, including:
  - six specially-commissioned film-based CPD units, written by Geoff Barton, with classroom lesson footage, additional interviews (with Phil Jarrett and Michelle Doran) and supporting written resources – ideal for departmental meetings
  - a SPAG guide for GCSE teaching
- Planning resources, including:
  - editable sample schemes of work and medium-term plans, with guidance on what to consider when planning your GCSE course
  - CPD units supporting discussion around departmental GCSE planning
- Digital books including:
  - all three Student Books in digital format*
  - a bank of tools enabling personalization

*Also available individually for student access

COMPONENT 1

Section A Reading

Introduction to Component 1, Section A Reading

Component 1 at a glance

Component 1
- 40% of total marks for GCSE English Language
- Assessment length: 1 hour 45 minutes
- Section A Reading
- Section B Writing

Section A Reading
- 20% of total grade
- Short and long answer questions
- 1 hour (10 minutes reading and 50 minutes answering questions)

What types of questions will be in Section A Reading?

Section A of Component 1 will test you on your ability to read and understand a piece of 20th-century literary prose writing. This means that you will be assessed on your understanding of an extract of narrative fiction (a story) which was published between 1900 and 1999.

Section A is worth half of the marks available for Component 1 and will be marked out of a total of 40 marks. As you will see elsewhere in this book, Section B Writing is also worth a total of 40 marks.

In Section A, you will be expected to answer a series of structured questions which will test your knowledge of the writer's meaning and how they have established that meaning.

Assessment Objectives

Section A: Reading of the Component 1 exam will test your abilities in the following assessment objectives (AOs):

AO1 Identify and interpret explicit and implicit information and ideas.

Select and synthesize evidence from different texts.

AO2 Explain, comment on and analyse how writers use language and structure to achieve effects and influence readers, using relevant subject terminology to support their views.

AO4 Evaluate texts critically and support this with appropriate textual references.

What is covered in this chapter?

This chapter will help you to prepare for the Reading section of the Component 1 exam. During the course of the chapter you will learn how to demonstrate a number of skills, which include how to:

- locate explicit and implicit ideas and details within a text
- interpret ideas
- make inferences based on information that has been gathered
- explore how writers use language
- explore how writers use structure
- explore how writers achieve effects
- explore how a writer can influence a reader
- give a personal response to or critical evaluation of what you have read.

Exam link

How will this chapter help me prepare for the exam?

In this chapter, you will be getting to know the Reading section of the Component 1 exam, known as Section A. In order to do this, you will first be given an explanation of how this part of the exam is structured. You will then carry out a range of activities which will help you understand the types of skills you will be expected to demonstrate in the exam, while also giving you plenty of opportunity to practise these skills. There will be tips on how to do your best in the exam and sometimes advice about things to avoid.

There are plenty of opportunities throughout each unit in this chapter for you to assess your own work and that of a classmate. Setting targets for improvement is part of an important process of 'plan–do–review', which will help you build on your strengths and tackle your weaknesses before the exam.

Good luck!

1 Location of explicit ideas and details

Assessment Objective

- **AO1**
  - 1a Identify explicit information.
  - 1b Identify explicit ideas.

The skill of locating **explicit** ideas and details means that you will need to find clearly and openly expressed details to prove or show something. The exam question may not always tell you that it is looking for explicit detail but might ask you what **evidence** or **details** you can find to prove something. The questions you will encounter in this unit are all designed to encourage you to demonstrate the **location** of explicit ideas and details and should give you an idea of how this type of question might be written in an exam.

- In an exam situation it is important that you read the text and the questions carefully.
  - Be aware of which lines or areas of text each question is asking you to look at, for example, 'paragraph 4' or 'the first 3 lines'. Make sure that your answer only uses evidence from those specific lines.
  - It is most sensible to read and 'track' through the text chronologically to make sure that you don't miss anything. Reading and answering chronologically will also make it easier to follow a writer's intentions and help you avoid confusing or misinterpreting what has been written.
- Make your points clearly and support them with evidence from the text.
- Show your powers of selection by choosing your quotation carefully. It is often not necessary to quote whole sentences. Focus instead on the particular words or phrases that enable you to make your point most clearly.

Key terms

Explicit: openly/exactly stated or expressed

Evidence: a fact or piece of information that gives a reason for believing something

Detail(s): individual fact(s) or feature(s)

Location: the exact place of something

Tip — Read smart – top tips

1. Read each question carefully at least twice before you read the specific lines from the extract that it is questioning you on.

2. When you are sure you know what the question is asking you, make a mark on your exam paper to indicate where you should stop reading for the question you are answering.

3. Read with the question in mind. Use a pen or highlighter as you read to pick out the key evidence that will help you answer the question.

4. Be specific. Only highlight the relevant words or phrases – too much underlining or highlighting will make it difficult to work out which evidence to use.

Activity 1

Read the following extract and then answer the question below:

List five details you learn about Emma Morley's
lifestyle.   **[5]**

Extract from *One Day* by David Nicholls

Emma Morley eats well and drinks in moderation. These days
she gets eight good hours sleep then wakes promptly of her own
accord at just before six-thirty and drinks a large glass of water, the
first 250ml of a daily 1.5 litres, which she pours from the brand new
5   carafe and matching glass that stand in a shaft of fresh morning
sunlight next to her warm, clean double bed. A carafe. She owns a
carafe. She can hardly believe it's true.

She owns furniture too. At twenty-seven she is too old to live like a
student anymore, and she now owns a bed, a large wrought-iron
10   and wickerwork affair bought in the summer sales from a colonial-
themed store on Tottenham Court Road. Branded the 'Tahiti' it
occupies the whole bedroom of her flat off the Earls Court Road.
The duvet is goosedown, the sheets are Egyptian cotton which
is, the saleswoman informed her, the very best cotton known to
15   man, and all of this signifies a new era of order, independence
and maturity.

The **[5]** at the end of the question in Activity 1 on page 13 indicates that this question is worth five marks. In an exam that means that you would score a mark for each relevant piece of evidence. If a question gives you the instruction to 'list' then you can present your answer using bullet points.

Mark your own answers to the question in Activity 1 and give yourself one mark (up to a total of five) for any of the following:

- Emma Morley 'eats well'.
- Emma Morley 'drinks in moderation'.
- She 'gets eight good hours sleep'.
- She wakes 'of her own accord at just before six-thirty'.
- She starts the day with a 250ml glass of water.
- She drinks 1.5 litres of water 'daily'.
- She pours her water from a 'brand new carafe and matching glass' which 'she owns'.
- She 'owns furniture', such as 'a large wrought-iron and wickerwork' bed.
- She is 'too old to live like a student'.
- She is experiencing 'a new era of order, independence and maturity'.

As you can see there are more than five points to make in relation to this question. In an exam if you can see or have picked out more points than you think you may need, it is always worth writing down one or two more to make absolutely sure of the 5 marks.

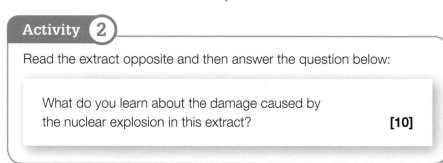

Activity 2

Read the extract opposite and then answer the question below:

What do you learn about the damage caused by the nuclear explosion in this extract? **[10]**

Extract from *Brother in the Land* by Robert Swindells

This extract is about a boy called Danny who is one of the few survivors of a nuclear holocaust. This is the beginning of his journey back to his home town after the explosion.

On the edge of town the houses were all burnt out, charred, glassless windows and caved-in roofs. Inside you could see wallpaper, fireplaces and bits of stairs going nowhere. Smoke rose thinly here and there
5 through blackened timbers.

[…] As I moved further into town the damage got worse. Some of the buildings had collapsed; drifts of smashed brick lay spilled across the road and I had to pick my way round them. There were more bodies,
10 and broken glass everywhere, some of it fused by heat into fantastic shapes. There were burnt out vehicles and the air smelled of charred wood.

Our shop was in the west part of town, the part farthest away from Branford. The worse devastation
15 was to the east. As I made my way westward the damage grew lighter and I began to hope that I might find my family unscathed and my home intact.

I saw people. Some were walking about. Others sat on steps, gazing at the ground in front of them. Nobody looked at me, or tried to speak. I felt invisible,   20
like a ghost.

Treading carefully between heaps of rubble and bits of glass I came to the top of my own street. Some of the houses still stood, others lay smashed. I could see from here that the shop was down.   25

I ran, in the middle of the road. My legs were weak with fear so that I almost fell.

The van lay on its side in the roadway, burnt out. The whole shop had collapsed though nearby houses still stood. I scrabbled among the rubble, calling brokenly   30
to my parents. I imagined them lying crushed or burned beneath the bricks and plaster and I started to dig with my bare hands; pulling out bricks and throwing them aside. Then a voice said, 'Danny?' and I spun round, still bent over with a brick in either hand. My dad was   35
standing by the cellar-steps, looking at me.

You will notice that the question on page 14 is worth 10 marks. You have not been told to list for this question and it would not be helpful to do so because some of the points you will locate in response may need to be explained. Read the sample answer to this question and the commentary below.

This is a reasonable overview point to make in response to the question. It does not identify any explicit information but it shows awareness and sets up the answer that will follow.

While this is true, we have already been told that there has been an explosion in the introduction to the text and in the question, so this demonstrates little knowledge of the damage or indeed the text.

This is more focused on detail but there are a number of specific details in relation to the surroundings appearing burned that could have been brought in here.

This is the best part of the answer. There is a focus on explicit information like the 'caved-in' roofs and the 'bits of stairs going nowhere' and it tries to show understanding of what these details mean.

This information is not needed to answer the question – it doesn't tell us anything about the damage caused by the explosion.

There is a lot of damage to the town that Danny sees on his way back to his shop. The town looks like there has been an explosion. Everything is burned like there has been a fire. Some of the roofs are 'caved-in' and this means you can see into the houses and see the wallpaper and that there are 'bits of stairs going nowhere'. It's like they have had the upstairs taken away and the stairs haven't got anywhere to go to. Danny's shop was in the west part of the town and not near Branford. His area wasn't as badly damaged and when he got there he was hoping that his family would be all right. He had to 'tread carefully through heaps of rubble and bits of glass' when he got to his own street which shows there was still some damage. Then he finds that the shop had been destroyed.

Again this is true but the information could have been more developed and clearly linked to evidence from the text.

How to improve

While the answer above makes some reasonable points it could go much further and demonstrate a clearer awareness of the question.

One of the points made by the answer above is that:

> Everything is burned like there has been a fire.

This could be improved as follows:

> It is clear that much of the town is 'burnt out' with increasing evidence pointing to 'charred' buildings that, in some cases, are still smoking and have 'blackened timbers'. The heat caused by the explosion was obviously intense as it was capable of fusing the 'broken glass' into 'fantastic shapes' and is also responsible for...

There is a lot of evidence in relation to the damage caused by the explosion on offer in this extract and much of it is overlooked by the answer on page 16. A better answer would present a greater range or selection of evidence. This means the answer would demonstrate awareness of several different but relevant points.

Activity 3

Bearing in mind the advice given, try to improve your own answer to this question.

What do you learn about the damage caused by the nuclear explosion in this extract?   [10]

Being able to identify and show you have understood explicit information in a fictional text is a very beneficial skill to learn. Not only are you tested on this particular skill in the exam, but it can also prove useful as a starting point for some of the skills you will practise later in this chapter.

Read the following extract and then complete the activity at the end which will help you to practise your location skills.

Extract from *The Fire-Eaters* by David Almond

This is an extract from the beginning of a story written from the perspective of a young boy called Bobby. On the day in question he has travelled with his mother into the city.

It all starts on the day I met McNulty. I was with my Mam. We left Dad at home beside the sea. We took the bus to Newcastle. We got out below the statue of the angel then headed down towards the market
5 by the river. She was all in red. She kept singing 'The Keel Row' and swinging my arm to the rhythm of the song. A crowd had gathered beyond the market stalls but we couldn't see what held so many people there. She led me closer. She stood on tiptoes. There
10 were bodies all around me, blocking out the light. Seagulls were squealing. It had been raining. There were puddles in the joints between the cobblestones. I kicked water across my shiny new black shoes. The splashes turned to dark stains on my jeans. The water
15 splashed on her ankles as well but she didn't seem to feel it. I tugged her hand and wanted to move away, but she didn't seem to feel it.

His voice was muffled by the bodies, and at first it seemed so distant. 'Pay!' he yelled. 'You'll not see
20 nowt till you pay!' I tugged her hand again. 'Are you not listening?' he yelled. I raised my eyes and tried to see. And she put her hands beneath my

arms and lifted me and I teetered on my toes and there he was, at the centre of us all. I looked into his eyes. He looked back into mine. And it was like 25
my heart stopped beating and the world stopped turning. That was when it started. That moment, that Sunday, late summer, 1962.

He was a small, wild-eyed, bare-chested man. His skin was covered in scars and bruises. There were 30
rough and faded tattoos of beasts and women and dragons. He had a little canvas sack on a long stick. He kept shoving it at the crowd.

'Pay!' he yelled and snarled. 'You'll not get nowt till you pay.' 35

Some of the crowd turned away and pushed past us as we moved forward. They shook their heads and rolled their eyes. He was pathetic, they said. He was a fake. One of them leaned close to Mam. 'Take the lad away,' he said. 'Some of the tricks is 40
just disgusting. Not for bairns to see. It shouldn't be allowed.'

McNulty's hair was black. He had pointed gold teeth at the front of his mouth and he wore tiny golden earrings. There were deep creases in his 45
cheeks. The bridge was high behind him. The sun shone through its arch. Steam and scents from the hot-dog stalls and popcorn-makers drifted across us. Mam held me against her.

Activity 4

You could be asked to locate explicit information or ideas about a number of different things in this extract. For example, you might be asked to find explicit details on one of the characters, or on the time and place.

Draw a table based on the one below. List all the explicit information you can find that relates to the different categories.

An example has been provided to start you off. Note – some points may fit into more than one category, so you should list those in every relevant place.

Narrator (Bobby)	Mam	Place or setting	McNulty	Crowd
He was travelling with his 'Mam'.	She was dressed 'all in red'.	'the market by the river'	He was a 'small, wild-eyed, bare-chested man'.	It was a dense crowd 'bodies all around... blocking out the light'.

Activity 5

Make a list of questions you might be asked for each of the categories in Activity 4 in order to test your skills in locating explicit information. These might be quite general or try to direct your focus to something specific.

For example:

> What do you learn about the crowd in these lines?

or

> What evidence can you find to show that there was a large crowd?

Activity 6

Choose one of your own questions to answer from Activity 5. You can select some of the relevant evidence from your table to help you with this.

Progress check

Swap your answer from Activity 6 with a partner and ask them to highlight three things they think you did well. For example, they may comment on effective use of quotation, your focus on the question or that you demonstrate a range of evidence. Then ask them to underline and comment on three areas where you could improve.

Reflect upon their comments before trying to answer one more of your questions from Activity 5. You should choose a question which relates to a different category.

2 Interpretation of ideas and details

Assessment Objective

- **AO1**
  – 1 Identify and interpret explicit and implicit information and ideas.

Key terms

Interpret: to explain the meaning of something said or written, or of someone's actions

Implicit: meaning that is suggested but not directly expressed

The skill of interpretation means working with explicit detail to demonstrate that you understand its full meaning, perhaps even making inferences about what you have read. A question which asks you to demonstrate location skills may offer two or three pieces of evidence which you can directly locate and use to answer the question, but it may also require you to stand back from the text and interpret what that evidence reveals.

For example, if you were asked to write about what you learn about a hopeless waiter in a text, you might use explicit information from the text to describe him (such as the fact that he is identified as late to work or carrying plates with his thumb resting in the dinner), but you might also come to the conclusion that he is clumsy because the writer describes him dropping things on more than one occasion. This is an **implicit** suggestion that he is uncoordinated.

The extract below is about a boy called Sean who lived in Ireland during the time of the potato famine. Read it carefully.

Extract from *Twist of Gold* by Michael Morpurgo

Sean suppressed the surge of excitement that bubbled within him as he approached the village. A fresh source of food was not something to be shared with anyone except his mother and his
5   sister, Annie. The village was silent, empty of people. Only the smoke from the chimneys betrayed any sign of life. But he knew they were all inside the cottages, those that had stayed, those that had survived. Every door was shut against the world. No dogs came out to bark at him, no children raced down the bracken track
10   from the church, no pigs snuffled in the fuchsia-covered ditches. The dust bowls by the churchyard gate were still there – mud-puddles in winter – but in summer all the hens and cockerels in the village used to congregate here for their ablutions and talk noisily as they wriggled and squirmed in the dust. Sean could not remember now when it was he last heard the cry of a cockerel.

A question you might be asked about this extract is:

> What do you learn about life in the village?   **[5]**

An answer to this question may include some of the following points:

Explicit information
- The village 'was silent'.
- The village appeared 'empty of people'.
- Everyone was 'inside the cottages' with their doors 'shut against the world'.
- Sean could see 'no dogs', 'no children', 'no pigs'.
- He couldn't hear any sounds of the 'hens and cockerels'.

Implicit details we learn by interpreting the evidence
- Sean can see few signs of life in the village.
- There is a sense that things have changed for the worse — the previously active behaviour of the barking dogs, racing children, snuffling pigs and noisy poultry is presented.
- Some people have gone away or died — he refers to 'those that had stayed' or 'survived' which implies some people hadn't.

By presenting explicit ideas in combination with some interpretation of the evidence it is possible to give a full and coherent answer. Try to avoid repeating yourself; instead you should build upon what you have written by linking the explicit information and the implicit meaning that can be revealed. Look at the following answers and work out which one is most effective.

Student ①

In the village we can see that there are no people: it is 'empty of people'. There was some smoke showing a 'sign of life' but there were no people to be seen. All the people were 'inside the cottages' so that is why there was no one to be seen. There were also no animals to be seen. There were 'no dogs ... to bark at him, no children raced down the bracken track, no pigs... in the fuchsia-covered ditches'. So there were no people and no animals anywhere and the only signs of life came from the chimneys.

Student ②

There is a sense that life in the village has changed in a negative way. Sean describes it as 'silent' and 'empty of people'. The sights that he would normally expect to see in the summer are not evident. There are 'no dogs', 'no children' and 'no pigs' to be seen. Similarly the normal sounds of 'hens and cockerels' who would 'talk noisily' are not evident and seemingly had been missing for some time as 'Sean could not remember' the last time he heard 'the cry of a cockerel'.

Activity ①

The answers above are both of similar length but one is more efficient and scores more highly than the other. Write down which one you think is better and explain why.

On the previous page the second answer was better and more efficient although both would have scored marks. They have been annotated with an examiner's commentary below so you can see what was achieved by each answer.

Student 1

Repeating the previous point – doesn't really add anything

This makes the point the student started with – the 'sign of life' quotation

Repetition of first point

This is a fair point but a lot of words are used to make it and the quotation is not really selective

Repeats the points that have already been made

In the village we can see that there are no people, it is 'empty of people'. ✓ There was some smoke showing a 'sign of life' but there were no people to be seen. All the people were 'inside the cottages' ✓ so that is why there was no one to be seen. There were also no animals to be seen. There were 'no dogs came out to bark at him, no children raced down the bracken track, no pigs... in the fuchsia-covered ditches'. ✓ So there were no people and no animals anywhere and the only signs of life came from the chimneys.

Student 1's answer shows awareness of the explicit detail in the extract and accumulates a few marks. It takes longer than it needs to for the student to make a point, though, and the answer is quite repetitive. It scored 3 marks.

Student 2

Immediately addresses the question and offers an interpretation of the evidence

Separates into two clear quotations in order to quickly make two distinct points

Offers an interpretation of the evidence

Picks out the important details and isolates them

Quickly links the next piece of evidence

Develops the point to demonstrate clearer awareness of meaning

There is a sense that life in the village has changed in a negative way. ✓ Sean describes it as 'silent' ✓ and 'empty of people'. ✓ The sights that he would normally expect to see in the summer are not evident. ✓ There are 'no dogs', 'no children' and 'no pigs' to be seen. ✓ Similarly the normal sounds of 'hens and cockerels' who would 'talk noisily' are not evident ✓ and seemingly had been missing for some time as 'Sean could not remember' the last time he heard 'the cry of a cockerel'. ✓

Student 2's answer is slightly shorter than the first one but wastes no words. There is a clear focus on the question and the evidence is quickly presented and examined. The student draws additional conclusions from the evidence to develop the range of evidence on offer. This answer scored 5 marks.

Activity 2

Read the extract below and then answer the following question:

> What do you learn about the relationship between the narrator's parents in this extract? **[5]**

Extract from *Travels with My Aunt* by Graham Greene

My father [...] was a building contractor of a lethargic disposition who used to take afternoon naps in all sorts of curious places. This irritated my mother, who was an energetic woman, and she used to seek him out to disturb him. As a child I remember going
5 to the bathroom – we lived in Highgate then – and finding my father asleep in the bath in his clothes. I am rather short-sighted and I thought that my mother had been cleaning an overcoat, until I heard my father whisper, 'Bolt the door on the inside when you go out.' He was too lazy to get out of the bath and too sleepy, I
10 suppose, to realize that his order was quite impossible to carry out. At another time, when he was responsible for a new block of flats in Lewisham, he would take his catnap in the cabin of the giant crane, and construction would be halted until he woke. My mother, who had a good head for heights, would climb ladders to
15 the highest scaffolding in the hope of discovering him, when as like as not he would have found a corner in what was to be the underground garage. I had always thought of them as reasonably happy together: their twin roles of the hunter and the hunted probably suited them.

Progress check

1. Share your answer with a partner.

    - Have you both covered the same points and chosen similar evidence?

    - Could anything your partner has found be added to your answer and vice versa?

2. Using different coloured highlighter pens, now indicate which points you have made that use explicit evidence from the text and which points required a little more interpretation of the evidence.

Tip Remember you are looking for details that specifically relate to the relationship between the parents. Try noting down what you discover in bullet points to see if any of the points can be related to one another or developed before writing your answer in full.

Look back at the advice given on page 12. Remember it is important to 'track' through the text chronologically to make sure that you don't miss anything. Make your points clearly and support them with carefully selected evidence from the text.

③ Looking at language

Assessment Objective

- **AO2**
  - 1a Comment on, explain and **analyse** how writers use language, using relevant subject terminology to support your views.

This unit will build upon the skills of locating, understanding and interpreting, and show you how to develop them further to focus on a writer's use of language. It is important that you are able to comment on and explain the different ways that a writer uses language in the material you read. There are a number of ways and levels at which this skill can be tested, but they will all require you to engage with and explore the way a writer uses words to create meaning.

Analysing language involves looking at the meaning, or layers of meaning, that have been created and exploring what the writer has done to create that meaning. A reader must engage with the words (phrases, sentences and so on) of a text in order to work out how a writer has:

- created impressions
- influenced a reader
- put forward a character's thoughts and feelings
- created particular effects.

Although AO2(1a) requires that you use 'relevant subject terminology' to support your views, this does not mean that you should fill each answer with meaningless technical vocabulary. Use technical terms only where you are confident in their meaning and are certain that they are beneficial to your point. Don't spend time searching for certain techniques in an exam in order to show that you have spotted them. Mental checklists of technical terminology are not always helpful and can lead you away from the task at hand.

The important point in this assessment objective is the word 'relevant' – if a writer has used imagery for effect and you recognize this, then go ahead and write it down – but be sure to explain *how* a writer has done that. Often, describing what you think a writer has done can show an awareness of a writer's method and that will gain you marks. For example, describing how a writer *lists* several negative aspects of a character's personality in order to build up evidence against them (and the careful selection of some of the evidence in that list) would show engagement with a writer's technique and use relevant subject terminology at the same time.

Activity 1

Read the extract on page 26 and complete the following table which will help you to answer the question:

> What impressions do you get of Patrick in these lines? **[10]**

What impression do you get of Patrick?	How is this impression created? What evidence do you have?
He is determined to upset his family with his last act.	His will was 'the final instrument of his anger against them'.
He puts great thought into how best to create offence.	He had the 'paranoiac's gift of investing everything with significance'.

Write down as many different impressions as you can. Be careful not to be too general – it would be easy to give the overall impression that Patrick is not a very nice man here, but that will only take you so far. Try to give more specific impressions you have of him as you track through the text.

Extract from *The Paperchase* by Marcel Theroux

Patrick hadn't forgotten the rest of his family: on the contrary, his will had been drawn up with a thoroughness that made me think it was the final instrument of his anger against them. Patrick had
5 the paranoiac's[1] gift of investing everything with significance. His other legacies were small and sardonic[2]: a pasta machine for an overweight sister (Judith); the complete works of Frederick Rolfe[3] for an illiterate and vulgar niece (Tricia); a mechanical
10 penny-bank for my father, whom Patrick had always considered covetous. He had amended the document constantly, according to his persecution mania, and whom he considered to be his current enemies. [...]

The last thing in the world that Patrick wanted was
15 for his family to benefit from his death. One way and another, he had fallen out with all of them, alienating them over the years with stinging letters or cold silences. He suffered from the worst kind of paranoia – the kind that has a firm basis in reality. Of course people talked about him behind his back. Of course 20 people avoided him. Of course people were afraid of him – to have any dealings with him whatsoever was to risk coming into conflict with him. And the most trivial disputes could engender letters so offensive that the insults would be burned on to your consciousness 25 for ever. 'You have all the attributes of a dog except fidelity,' he wrote to an ex-girlfriend. He once told my kindly Aunt Judith she was a two-hundred-pound puff adder[4].

[1] paranoiac – someone who suffers from paranoia – an unjustified suspicion and mistrust of other people
[2] sardonic – humorous in a grim or sarcastic way
[3] Frederick Rolfe – an English author writing in the late 1800s and early 1900s
[4] puff adder – a large poisonous snake

Activity 2

Use your table to try to answer the question in Activity 1.
Think very carefully about the way you present your evidence.
Make sure you show how the evidence you have chosen creates
the impression you suggest. For example:

> I get the impression that Patrick is determined to upset his family
> with his last act, the writing of his will. The narrator describes it as
> 'the final instrument of his anger against them'. This comparison
> makes it seem like a specific and carefully chosen tool that he is
> using precisely and for maximum effect. It is almost like he is using
> it as a weapon and he means to have the last word.

• Immediate focus on the question and an impression given

• Supported by relevant evidence

• Relevant terminology – you might also use the word 'metaphor'

• Focus on exploring the language

• Some development of ideas

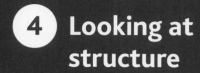

4 Looking at structure

Assessment Objective

- **AO2**
  – 1b Comment on, explain and analyse how writers use structure, using relevant subject terminology to support your views.

This unit will show you how to demonstrate your skills when looking at a writer's use of structure. It is important that you are able to comment on and explain the different ways that a writer uses structure and organizes a piece of writing in the material you read. In an exam you will do this at the same time as you discuss a writer's use of language, and the ways in which a writer might create effect, but in order to understand this skill better you will first look at it in isolation.

When you refer to the structure of a text or piece of fictional writing you will be commenting on the way in which the writing has been organized. A story does not begin as a series of random sentences and words on a page – the writer deliberately organizes and positions the words, phrases, sentences and paragraphs to create meaning and effect.

As with the work on a writer's use of language, AO2(1b) requires you to use relevant subject terminology to support your views. Once again, this needs to be meaningful in the way that you do it. For example, showing that you can identify a short sentence is not at all helpful unless you can explain that the short sentence was used deliberately by a writer and give reasons for this.

> **Activity** **1**
>
> Read the following extract and think about the way in which the writer organizes this part of the text.

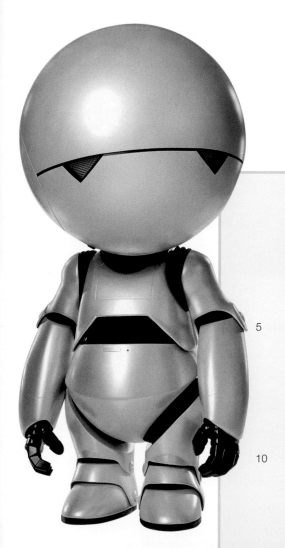

Extract from *The Restaurant at the End of the Universe* by Douglas Adams

Marvin stood at the end of the bridge corridor. He was not in fact a particularly small robot. His silver body gleamed in dusty sunbeams and shook with the continual barrage which the building was still undergoing.

He did, however, look pitifully small as the gigantic black tank rolled to a halt in
5 front of him. The tank examined him with a probe. The probe withdrew.

Marvin stood there.

'Out of my way, little robot,' growled the tank.

'I'm afraid,' said Marvin, 'that I've been left here to stop you.'

The probe extended again for a quick recheck. It withdrew again.

10 'You? Stop me?' roared the tank. 'Go on!'

'No, really I have,' said Marvin simply.

'What are you armed with?' roared the tank in disbelief.

'Guess,' said Marvin.

The tank's engines rumbled, its gears ground. Molecule-sized electronic relays

15 deep in its micro-brain flipped backwards and forwards in consternation.

'Guess?' said the tank. [...]

'Yes, go on,' said Marvin to the huge battle machine, 'you'll never guess.'

20 'Errrmmm...' said the machine, vibrating with unaccustomed thought, 'laser beams?'

Marvin shook his head solemnly.

'No,' muttered the machine in its deep guttural rumble, 'Too obvious. Anti-matter ray?' it hazarded.

25 'Far too obvious,' admonished Marvin.

'Yes,' grumbled the machine, somewhat abashed. 'Er... how about an electron ram?'

This was new to Marvin.

'What's that?' he said.

30 'One of these,' said the machine with enthusiasm.

From its turret emerged a sharp prong which spat a single lethal blaze of light. Behind Marvin a wall roared and collapsed as a heap of dust. The dust billowed brlefly, then settled.

35 'No,' said Marvin, 'not one of those.'

'Good though, isn't it?'

'Very good,' agreed Marvin.

'I know,' said the Frogstar battle machine, after another moment's consideration, 'you must have one of those

40 new Xanthic Re-Structron Destabilized Zenon Emitters!'

'Nice, aren't they?' said Marvin.

'That's what you've got?' said the machine in considerable awe.

'No,' said Marvin.

'Oh,' said the machine, disappointed, 'then it must be...' 45

'You're thinking along the wrong lines,' said Marvin. 'You're failing to take into account something fairly basic in the relationship between men and robots.'

'Er, I know,' said the battle machine, 'is it...' it tailed off into thought again. 50

'Just think,' urged Marvin, 'they left me, an ordinary, menial robot, to stop you, a gigantic heavy-duty battle machine, whilst they ran off to save themselves. What do you think they would leave me with?' 55

'Oooh er,' muttered the machine in alarm, 'something pretty damn devastating, I should expect.'

'Expect!' said Marvin, 'oh yes, expect. I'll tell you what they gave me to protect myself with shall I?'

'Yes, all right,' said the battle machine, bracing itself. 60

'Nothing,' said Marvin.

There was a dangerous pause.

'*Nothing?*' roared the battle machine.

'Nothing at all,' intoned Marvin dismally, 'not an electronic sausage.' 65

Typical questions you might be asked in response to this extract include:

How does the writer make these lines tense and/or dramatic?　**[10]**

or

How does the writer encourage you to feel sympathy for Marvin?　**[10]**

Obviously, there is lots of detail in relation to the content and language which would help you to answer these questions. For now, though, you need to think specifically about what points could be made about this extract in relation to structure. When commenting on structure it is essential to read a text chronologically – details deliberately come in the order intended by the writer.

Key terms

Dialogue: the words spoken by characters in a play, film or story

Question: a sentence that asks for information or an answer

Anti-climax: a disappointing ending to a series of events that seemed to be leading to a point of great interest or excitement

Activity 2

Track through the text on pages 28–29 and answer the following questions:

1. In the opening lines, why do you think the writer makes it clear that Marvin is not 'a particularly small robot' *before* telling us that he looked 'pitifully small' as the black tank pulled in front of him?

2. This extract is set out as **dialogue**. What does that mean?

3. Who is the dialogue between here?

4. What do you think the effect is of using dialogue in this extract?

5. Why has the writer used the sentence 'Marvin stood there' and positioned it in the way that he has?

6. The tank then asks Marvin **questions** such as 'You? Stop me?' and 'What are you armed with?' What impressions does the writer create of the tank by making it ask such questions?

7. When the black tank begins to list all of the weapons Marvin could have (for example, 'laser beams' or 'anti-matter ray') how does this affect the tension?

8. How does Marvin use **anti-climax** in response to the tank's assumption that he must have 'one of those new Xanthic Re-Structron Destabilized Zenon Emitters'?

9. What does Marvin say towards the end of this extract to summarize the different positions of the two participants in this conversation?

10. Can you connect this to the way they were introduced?

11. How does the ending make you feel sorry for Marvin?

12. How does the structure create tension at the end?

The writer of this extract teases the reader by revealing information quite slowly through a question and answer session between these two characters. He deliberately misleads or creates confusion through the structure in order to create tension. You may well have read this extract expecting Marvin to be destroyed at the end, or certainly disregarded as the black tank went on. This is what actually happened:

Extract from *The Restaurant at the End of the Universe* by Douglas Adams

The machine heaved about with fury.

'Well, doesn't that just take the biscuit!' it roared.

'Nothing, eh? Just don't think, do they?'

'And me,' said Marvin in a soft low voice, 'with this
5 terrible pain in all the diodes down my left side.'

'Makes you spit, doesn't it?'

'Yes,' agreed Marvin with feeling.

'Hell that makes me angry,' bellowed the machine, 'think I'll smash that wall down!'

10 The electron ram stabbed out another searing blaze of light and took out the wall next to the machine.

'How do you think I feel?' said Marvin bitterly.

'Just ran off and left you, did they?' the machine thundered.

'Yes,' said Marvin.   15

'I think I'll shoot down their bloody ceiling as well!' raged the tank.

It took out the ceiling of the bridge.

'That's very impressive,' murmured Marvin

'You ain't seen nothing yet,' promised the machine,   20
'I can take out this floor too, no trouble!'

It took out the floor too.

'Hell's bells!' the machine roared as it plummeted fifteen storeys and smashed itself to bits on the ground below.   25

'What a depressingly stupid machine,' said Marvin and trudged away.

Activity ③

Answer the following question:

How does the writer use structure to make this an effective ending to the whole passage?

You should comment on:

- how the dialogue is organized
- how the extract develops
- the release of key information.   **[10]**

5 Looking at how writers achieve effects

Assessment Objective

- **AO2**
  – 1c Comment on, explain and analyse how writers achieve effects, using relevant subject terminology to support your views.

This unit will focus on how a writer achieves effects. The use of language and structure are integral to a discussion of how a writer creates effect. You will be pulling together your skills in both areas as you think about how a writer has used them for effect.

The dictionary tells us that an 'effect' is:

| 'An impression produced in the mind of a person' | or | 'A change which is the result of an action or other cause' |

A writer achieves effects by creating impressions in the mind of the reader. They may write to change, confirm or develop your thinking. This can be achieved in many different ways – the writer may tell us things and influence us through the suggestions they make. The writer can also achieve effects by appealing to us descriptively and trying to influence our senses. In order to explain and analyse how writers achieve effects you need to comment on the ways writers deliberately use words and literary devices to create impressions.

Activity

Read the first extract from *Resistance* by Owen Sheers on page 33. Complete the table below as you think about the following question:

This extract marks the beginning of a significant change in Sarah's life. How does the writer prepare us for this change? **[10]**

Evidence	Effect
'For Sarah Lewis it began in her sleep.'	The use of the word 'it' provokes curiosity — the writer makes us wonder what began.
The 'drag', 'rattle' and 'bark' of the dogs 'straining on their chains'	The writer appeals to the senses with ominous sounding noises. We get the sense that the animals are unsettled and the fact that this intrudes into Sarah's dreams creates the idea that her sleep is also unsettled.
Her dream appears to be about 'a ship in a storm' with sailors 'shouting for help'	
The noise became like 'Marley's ghost, dragging his shackles over a flagstone floor'	'dragging his shackles' creates the impression that something sinister is about to happen. The use of 'Marley's ghost' also suggests that something may be about to change in the same way that his introduction was the beginning of Scrooge's transformation in *A Christmas Carol*.
'Clink, *slump*, clink, *slump*.'	
'Eventually, as the light brightened…'	
'the sound became what it was…'	
'Two dogs, urgent and distressed'	
'pulling again and again…'	

Extract 1 from *Resistance* by Owen Sheers

For Sarah Lewis it began in her sleep. The drag, rattle and bark of the dogs straining on their chains was so persistent it entered her dreams. A ship in storm, the sailors shouting for help from the
5   deck, their pink faces and open mouths obscured by the spray blown up the sides of the hull. Then the noise became Marley's ghost*, dragging his shackles over a flagstone floor. Clink, *slump*, clink, *slump*. Eventually, as the light brightened about the
10   edges of the blackout curtain and Sarah surfaced through the layers of her sleep, the sound became what it was. Two dogs, urgent and distressed, pulling again and again on their rusty chains and barking, short and sharp through the constraint of
15   their collars.

*Marley's ghost – a character that appears in Charles Dickens's *A Christmas Carol*. He is the first in a series of spirits who visit the character of Scrooge before Scrooge makes significant changes in his life. Marley has spent several years wrapped in heavy chains and wandering the Earth as a ghost in punishment for his previous sins.

Activity ②

Now read the next part of the extract. Think about the following question:

> How does the writer create the impression that this day is out of the ordinary?   **[10]**

Extract 2 from *Resistance* by Owen Sheers

Without opening her eyes Sarah slid her hand across the sheet behind her, feeling for the warm impression of her husband's body. The old horsehair mattress they slept on could hold the shape of a man all day
5   and although Tom was usually up before her, she found comfort in touching the warm indentation of where he'd lain beside her. She stroked her palm over the thin cotton sheet. A few hairs poking through the mattress caught against her skin, hard and stubborn
10   as the bristles on a sow's back.

And there he was. A long valley where his weight had pressed the ball of his shoulder and his upper arm into the bed; a rise where his neck had lain beneath the pillow. She explored further down. A deeper bowl
15   again, sunk by a protruding hip and then the shallower depression of his legs tapering towards the foot of the bed. As usual, Tom's shape, the landscape of him, was there. But it was cold. Normally Sarah could still feel the last traces of his body's heat, held in the fabric of the sheet just as the mattress held his form. But this   20 morning that residue was missing.

[…] She rose quickly, hoping movement would dispel her mild unease. Tugging roughly on the heavy blankets she made the bed, tucking their edges under the mattress. Then she plumped the pillows, shaking   25 them as if to wake them. Brushing a few of Tom's hairs from the one beside hers she paused for a second and stilled herself, as if the hairs might summon Tom himself. She listened, one hand still resting on the pillow. But there was nothing. Just the usual ticks and   30 groans of the old building waking and warming, and outside, the dogs, barking and barking.

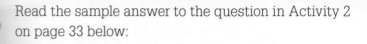

Read the sample answer to the question in Activity 2 on page 33 below:

> How does the writer create the impression that this day is out of the ordinary? **[10]**

Student 1

The writer creates the impression that something is wrong by making it seem as though Sarah does not feel what she expects to ✓ when she slides 'her hand across the sheet behind her'. She expects to feel warm sheets from where her husband was lying there but she doesn't because they are 'cold'. The writer makes this seem odd and not normal. She is feeling 'mild unease' but tries to get rid of this by getting on with the morning jobs. ✓ The house sounds normal, 'usual ticks and groans of a building waking and warming', except for the sound of the dogs ✓ who were 'barking and barking'.

Sensible comments

Teacher's comment

This is a reasonable answer – it makes some appropriate selection of detail in combination with two or three sensible comments. The answer ignores some of the important detail, though, and does not really explore how the writer's use of language helps to create effect.

Below is the first part of a more detailed answer to the same question. Read it carefully:

Student 2

The writer creates the impression that something is wrong by offering a vivid contrast between a usual beginning to a day for Sarah and what takes place on this day. Most of her actions are the same as usual but the few subtle differences alert us to the fact that something is wrong. Sarah reaches out in her normal way to feel the 'impression of her husband's body' in the mattress. We know that she generally 'found comfort' in touching the 'warm indentation' of where he had been lying. Her search reveals that although the 'landscape' of Tom is there 'as usual', on this occasion 'it was cold'. This difference in temperature creates a slight sense of unease rather than the normal 'comfort' Sarah would find there. Also, the writer creates the effect that he has been gone from the bed for some time, more time than he usually would have been, by his side of the bed being cold. The fact that 'Normally Sarah could still feel the last traces of his body's heat' heightens the contrast between her usual morning and this one.

Activity 3

Below are Student 2's notes on how they planned to complete the rest of their answer. Use these to write the conclusion of this answer yourself.

1. Make a point about Sarah's exploring of the bed – the 'valley' from the 'ball of his shoulder', the 'bowl' from his hip, the 'shallower depression of his legs'. All holes, spaces left, and emphasize the fact that he's not there.

2. Sarah tries to get on with a normal morning despite 'mild unease'.

3. Actions emphasize brisk and purposeful movement of normal morning – 'tugging roughly', 'tucking', 'plumped the pillows' contrasts with momentary pause because of hair.

4. Sarah 'listened' – trying to hear something out of the ordinary?

5. Normal house noises 'ticks and groans of the old building' but these contrast with 'the dogs, barking and barking'.

Tip You can only analyse the effect of the language you are presented with – trying to guess at what comes next in a piece of writing can lead to exam disaster. Try to avoid unsupported assertions (telling the examiner things that you cannot prove) and commentary that is speculative (guesswork). The following answer is almost complete guesswork and did not do well in response to this question:

The writer creates the impression that something is wrong and that Sarah's husband is dead or that he is about to die. By describing the empty bed where he once lay as 'cold' this foreshadows the fact that he will die because bodies are cold when the blood stops pumping around them. The fact that the dogs are 'barking and barking' also proves this because animals are able to sense when something is wrong and they can tell that something bad has happened to their master.

There is no proof of this in the extract you have read.

This is guesswork – there is no clear evidence to suggest this.

There is no way of knowing what the animals may or may not be able to tell.

6 Looking at how writers influence readers

This unit will focus on how a writer uses language to influence the reader.

A writer uses the tools at their disposal to influence their readers. The writer will use language to put forward ideas, play with and provoke a reader's senses and to emotionally engage a reader. A piece of writing may be tense and dramatic, funny and lively, or provoke sadness and empathy. It may also work on or affect any other human emotion you can think of. This unit will focus on how a writer is able to influence a reader through language and technique.

Read the following extract carefully. It is narrated by Kate who recalls an important moment from when she was a child. It begins at the point when she was at home with her younger sister Bo and her older brothers Matt and Luke. Matt and Luke were looking after the girls while their parents were out on a shopping trip.

Assessment Objective

- **AO2**

  1d – Comment on, explain and analyse how writers influence readers, using relevant subject terminology to support your views.

Extract from *Crow Lake* by Mary Lawson

It must have been the first time we'd been for a swim together, all four of us. The lake was less than twenty yards from the house so you just went in when you felt like it and I suppose we'd never all felt like it at

5 the same time before. In any case, my mother would always have taken Bo. But we passed her around between us, using her as a beach ball, and it was good fun. I remember that.

[…] I took my bathing suit outside to hang it on the

10 line, so I was the one to see the police car come down the drive.

You didn't often see police cars in Crow Lake and I was curious. I ran down to the driveway to look at it, and the policeman got out and to my surprise so

15 did Reverend Mitchell and Dr Christopherson. Rev. Mitchell was our minister and his daughter Janie was my best friend. […] I skipped up to them and said, 'Mum and Dad aren't here right now. They went shopping. They went to get a new suitcase for Luke,

20 because he's going to be a teacher.'

The policeman was standing by his car, looking intently at a small scratch on the fender. Rev. Mitchell looked at Dr Christopherson and then back at me and said, 'Is Luke here, Katherine? Or Matt?'

'They're both here,' I said. 'They're getting changed. 25 We've been for a swim.'

'We'd like a word with them. Could you tell them we're here?'

'OK,' I said. And then remembering my manners, 'Do you want to come in? Mum and Dad will be back 30 about half-past six.' I had a happy thought. 'I could make you a cup of tea.'

'Thank you,' Rev. Mitchell said. 'We'll come in, but I don't think… tea, thank you. Not right at the moment.'

I led them into the house and excused the noise Bo 35 was making – she'd got all the pots and pans out of the bottom cupboard and was bashing about with them on the kitchen floor. They said it didn't matter so I left them in the dining room while I went to get Luke and Matt. I brought them both back and they 40 looked curiously at the two men – the policeman had stayed by his car – and said hi. And then I saw Matt's face change. He'd been looking at Rev. Mitchell and suddenly he didn't look polite and curious any more. He looked afraid. 45

He said, 'What?'

Dr Christopherson said, 'Kate, I wonder if you could go and see to Bo? Could you just… um…?'

50 I went out to the kitchen. Bo wasn't doing anything wrong but I picked her up and carried her outside. She was getting big but I could still just carry her. I took her back down to the beach. The mosquitoes were starting to come out but I stayed there anyway, even when Bo began to rage at me, because I was 55 afraid of the expression on Matt's face and I didn't want to know what had caused it.

After a long time, half an hour at least, Matt and Luke came down to the beach. I didn't look at them. Luke picked Bo up and carried her down to the water's 60 edge and began to walk along the shore with her. Matt sat down beside me, and when Luke and Bo were a long way down the curve of the shore he told me that our parents had been killed when their car was hit by a fully loaded logging truck whose brakes failed as it was coming down Honister Hill. 65

***

I remember being terrified that he would cry. His voice was shaking and he was struggling very hard with himself, and I remember being rigid with fear, not daring to look at him, scarcely daring to breathe. As if that would be the worst thing; much worse than this 70 incomprehensible thing he was telling me. As if for Matt to cry was the one unthinkable thing.

On pages 36–37 we have presented slightly more of the extract than you would usually be required to comment on in answer to one question. This is in order to provide more opportunities for practice.

Activity

An exam question you might be set on key lines from this extract is:

> How does the writer make this part of the story powerful and dramatic? **[10]**

1. In order to answer this you need to think carefully about how the writer's use of language influences you as a reader. The table below tracks through the various stages of this extract. Copy the table and in each column write at least two or three pieces of evidence. The first one is done as an example for you.

2. Compare your table with a partner. Can you add to or develop any of the points you have made as a result of sharing your work?

At first everything seems to be fine	There is the sense that something is not right	Matt and Luke speak to the visitors but the situation is not clear	The news is tragic and shocking	The situation at the end is heartbreaking
They all went swimming together.	A police car arrives.	Matt's expression changes from 'polite' to 'afraid'.	'our parents had been killed when their car was hit'	Kate's focus is on her terror that Matt will cry.

Activity 2

In pairs, choose three pieces of evidence that you would use in an answer to the question in Activity 1. Discuss and make notes on how you will examine that evidence to show the effect it has on a reader. Try to stretch yourselves with your explanation and develop your ideas together.

For example, you might decide to focus on the arrival of the police car. You might set out your thinking as follows:

- Kate surprised at police car arrival — e.g. 'You didn't often see police cars in Crow Lake'. Kate was 'curious' — makes reader uneasy as police cars don't tend to bring good news

- Situation becomes stranger as Reverend Mitchell and Dr Christopherson get out

- Reader concerned at this point — recognizes there is something the writer isn't telling us

- Kate's reaction is innocent, she 'skipped up to them' — contrast between this innocence and what the reader suspects

Activity 3

Using all of the notes you have made so far, write a full response to the question in Activity 1.

7 Combining a writer's skills

Assessment Objective

- **AO2**
  – Explain, comment on and analyse how writers use language and structure to achieve effects and influence readers, using relevant subject terminology to support your views.

This unit will focus on combining the skills you have demonstrated over the last few units in order to look at the writer's craft as a whole. You will consider how writers use language and structure to achieve effects and influence readers.

The last few units have focused on the individual parts of the writer's craft:

- how writers use language
- how writers use structure
- how writers achieve effects
- how writers influence readers.

As each unit explained, these skills do not work alone. You are likely to need to comment on a combination of these details in order to do well in an exam.

Read the following summary of what you have learned between pages 12 and 39:

Recap on how writers use language and structure to achieve effects and influence readers

1. In looking at language you need to study how a writer has used words and phrases to create meaning.

2. The structure of a piece of writing is the way in which the words, sentences and paragraphs have been ordered. A writer deliberately organizes their writing to influence meaning and its effect.

3. The effect created by a writer refers to the way words and devices are deliberately used to create an impression or develop the thinking of the reader.

4. A writer uses their writing tools (language, structure, devices, etc.) to influence a reader. Think about how they use those tools to influence the way a reader may respond to or engage with the text.

Activity

Skim back through pages 12 to 39 and see if there is anything you would want to add to the revision notes on this page.

Read the following extract:

Extract from *Bluebeard's Egg and Other Stories* by Margaret Atwood

The raft was black and enormous, and seemed, resting at its moorings, very stable. Emma was given an orange life jacket, and buckled herself into it, helped by Bill. [...] Emma began to feel slightly let
5 down and to wonder why she'd come. The raft was too big, too solid; it was like a floating parking lot.

But once they'd moved out into the current, the rubber surface under her began to ripple, in large waves of contraction, like a giant throat swallowing,
10 and spray came in upon them, and Emma knew that the rapids, which had looked so decorative, so much like cake frosting from a distance, were actual after all. There were some dutiful thrilled noises from the other passengers, and then some genuine noises,
15 less thrilled. Emma found herself clutching Bill's arm, a thing she wouldn't ordinarily have done. The sky was an unnatural blue, and the shore – dotted with the white-clad or pastel figures of tourists, which appeared static and painted, like a design on
20 wallpaper – was very far away.

There was a lot of talk later about why the tenth run should have failed so badly, after the other nine had gone without a hitch. [...] Emma could not remember wondering why, at the time. All she saw was the front
25 of the raft tipping down into a trough deeper than any they'd yet hit, while a foaming wall of water rose above them. The raft should have curved sinuously, sliding up the wave. Instead it buckled across the middle, the front half snapping towards the back, like the beak of a bird closing. Emma and Bill and the other people in the 30 front row shot backwards over the heads of the rest, who were jumbling in a heap at the bottom of the V, now submerging. [...]

Something struck her on the side of the head – a foot in a boot, perhaps – and she was underwater. 35 Later she learned that the raft had flipped and a man had been trapped underneath it and drowned, so it was just as well that she had been flung clear. But underwater she did not think. Something else made her hold her breath and struggle towards the surface, 40 which she could see above her, white and silver, so her eyes must have been open. Her head rose up, she gasped air and was sucked under.

The water tumbled and boiled and Emma fought it. She was filled almost to bursting with an energy that 45 came from anger: *I refuse to die in such a stupid way*, was how she formulated this afterwards. She thinks she shouted, at least once: 'No!' Which was a waste of breath, as there was nobody around to hear her. There were rocks, and she collided with several 50 and was bruised and scraped, but nothing more hit her head, and after what seemed like an hour but was really only ten minutes the current was less and she found she could keep her head above the water and actually swim. It was hard to move her arms. 55 She propelled herself towards the shore, and, finally, dragged herself up onto a small rocky beach.

Activity ②

A question you might be set on this extract is:

> How does the writer develop a sense of drama in this extract? **[10]**

Before you write an answer to this question, re-read the extract and highlight or make a list of the evidence you could use. As you are doing this, consider whether you could discuss any of the following techniques as part of your answer:

- the effect created by the comparison between appearance and reality
- the dramatic effect of the writer's use of images
- the effect of the writer's choice of verbs
- how the writer creates a sense of Emma's helplessness
- the effect of the use of speech
- the way the writer presents time – real time/ remembered events.

These are just *some* ideas you may wish to develop. Make sure you do not just simply identify points. Try to explain how they work to create drama.

8 Personal/ critical evaluation

Assessment Objective

● **AO4**
  – **Evaluate** texts critically and support this with appropriate textual references.

Key terms

Critical: independent study and evaluation in order to form a judgement
Evaluate: to form an idea of; to assess and decide a value
Judgement: a considered decision or sensible conclusion

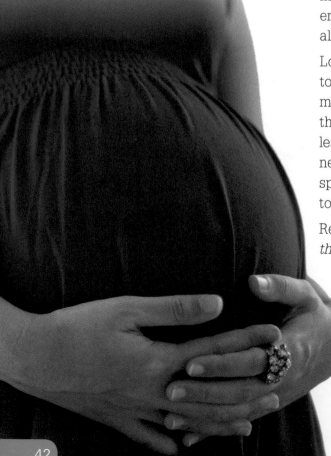

A personal or **critical** evaluation involves explaining and exploring your own response as a reader. It is partly to do with your personal feelings about the way a story or a character develops, but you will need to do more than express simple feelings of like and dislike. You are required to explain and analyse what a writer does in order to make you respond as you do. The more specifically you can identify your own reactions the better. In effect, you need to use evidence from the text in order to make sensible conclusions about your own response to what you have read.

When you are asked to make a personal response to or **judgement** on a text (or an extract from a text) the examiner will be looking to see whether you can assess what you have been reading and come to a sensible judgement about it. The examiner will also be looking to see whether you can explain how the writer led you to that judgement.

Once again, tracking through the text is an essential skill. Although writing about the text in the same order that the writer presents it is always sensible in terms of the organization and coherence of your answer, it has added benefits when focusing on your own response. A writer may be writing to try to affect or manipulate your response through the structure of the text – information may be revealed in a particular order for that very reason. Tracking through the text will make sure that your response follows the sequence of events and enables you to make sure that you do not miss vital clues which may alter or affect your reactions.

Look at the definitions in the key terms box. You may be more used to seeing these words in a different environment; perhaps they sound more like the kinds of words used in Science or Maths. In English, these terms are used slightly differently because you are studying less obvious things such as feelings and reactions, but the steps you need to take to explore them are similar. You will need to focus on specific detail and examine evidence in order to show how you came to a judgement.

Read the following extract from the beginning of the novel *Red Sky in the Morning*.

Extract from *Red Sky in the Morning* by Elizabeth Laird

As long as I live, I shall never forget the night my brother was born. For one thing, I didn't get a wink of sleep. I'd only been in bed a few minutes when I heard Dad talking on the telephone. My bedroom's pretty

5 small, and if I lean out of bed far enough I can open the door without actually getting out of bed, so I did, and I heard Dad say,

'That's right, the second house on the left past the shops. And please hurry.'

10 His voice sounded so urgent I guessed at once he must be calling the ambulance and I knew my time had come. Well, it was Mum's time really, but mine too, in a way, because I was going to be in charge while she was away. I'd practised everything in my

15 mind, so I just got calmly out of bed, and put on my dressing gown, and groped around for my glasses. Then I went calmly out of the room and walked down the hall to Mum and Dad's bedroom. I didn't even run.

'Now just relax, Mum,' I said. 'Everything's under

20 control.' I must have said it too calmly because no one took any notice. Mum's face was screwed up, and

Mum's face went ordinary again, and she turned her head and saw me, and she looked quite normal. In fact, she gave me a smile. Then Dad started pulling on his trousers again. It was like starting up a video again 25 after a freeze frame.

After that, everything I'd planned to say was swept out of my head, because things happened too fast. Mum's face screwed up again, and she started taking loud, rasping breaths. I've never seen such an awful look in 30 anyone's eyes, not even in a war film.

Dad grabbed his jacket, and pushed past me out of the room. Then I suppose he must have realized it was me, because he came back and ruffled my hair the way he does when he wants to be nice to me. I hate 35 it, but I don't like hurting his feelings, so I just suffer in silence.

'Be a nice girl,' he said. 'Go and get me a cup of tea. The ambulance won't be here for another five minutes. I've got to go and phone your granny.' 40

I couldn't believe it. I've never heard anything so callous in all my life. There was his wife, probably dying, in the most awful agony, trying to give birth to his own child, and all he could think of were his own selfish pleasures. I realized how woman has suffered 45 from man's selfishness since time began.

'Sorry, Dad,' I said with dignity. 'I expect Mum needs me. You'll find the tea in the usual place.'

Activity **1**

A question you might be asked in relation to the extract on page 43 is:

> How do you react to what takes place in these lines? **[10]**

We are introduced very quickly to the events that are to take place in the extract. The narrator (Anna) is about to become a big sister. Interestingly, however, our reactions may not mirror hers. Copy and complete the following table to demonstrate how you react to her and the situation that she is in. You need to think about what she says and what she does. Try to draw sensible conclusions from the evidence.

Evidence	Reader's reaction	Explanation
'As long as I live, I shall never forget the night my brother was born.'	A memorable night	Emphasized by 'as long as I live' — we get the sense that this is a memory that will never fade. The reader may feel anxious at this point. Is the narrator emotionally scarred? Is it a happy memory?
'I didn't get a wink of sleep.'		
'His voice sounded so urgent...'		
'I knew my time had come.'		This makes me feel curious and a little amused/engaged by the character. She is a child herself but seems to think she has an important role to play.
'I was going to be in charge while she was away...'		
'I'd practised everything in my mind...'	She had obviously been thinking about this.	
repetition of 'calmly': 'I just got calmly out of bed'/ 'I went calmly out of the room'		
'I didn't even run.'		
'"Now just relax, Mum," I said. "Everything's under control."'		
'No one took any notice.'		
'Mum's face was screwed up...'		Child's blunt perspective on the agony her mum must be experiencing. This makes me realize she has no idea of the real seriousness of the situation.

'Dad was looking at her, standing quite still, with one leg in his trousers and the other out.'		Situation must be serious
'He looked perfectly ridiculous.'		
'It was like starting up a video again after a freeze frame.'		
'...everything I'd planned to say was swept out of my head, because things happened too fast.'		
'I've never seen such an awful look in anyone's eyes, not even in a war film.'		
'Dad grabbed his jacket, and pushed past me out of the room.'		
'...he came back and ruffled my hair the way he does when he wants to be nice to me.'		
"Go and get me a cup of tea... I've got to go and phone your granny."		This is not what she thinks. I think he's trying to find her a job so that she moves away from her mum's room and feels useful at the same time.
'I've never heard anything so callous in all my life.'		
'I realised how woman has suffered from man's selfishness since time began.'	Amused	
'"Sorry, Dad," I said with dignity. "I expect Mum needs me. You'll find tea in the usual place."'		

Activity 2

Now try to answer the question in Activity 1. Time yourself – you only have 15 minutes.

Tip You can write quite a lot in 15 minutes but you may need to prioritize which points you wish to use from the table. If more than one piece of evidence has produced a similar response from you then you may wish to combine those points to make sure you have time to discuss a range of reactions.

Activity

Read the following extract carefully and then answer the question below:

'In this passage the writer encourages the reader to feel dislike towards Enno Kluge.'

To what extent do you agree with this view?

You should write about:

- your own impressions of Enno as he is presented here
- how the writer has created these impressions. **[10]**

Extract from *Alone in Berlin* by Hans Fallada

This extract is about Eva Kluge, a postwoman living in Germany during the time of the Second World War.

Eva Kluge finished her delivery round at two o'clock. She then worked till four totting up newspaper rates and surcharges: if she was very tired, she got her numbers muddled up and she would have to start again. Finally, with sore feet and a painful vacancy
5 in her brain, she set off home; she didn't want to think about everything she had to do before getting to bed. On the way home, she shopped, using her ration cards. There was a long line at the butcher's, and so it was almost six when she slowly climbed the steps to her apartment on Friedrichshain.

10 On her doorstep stood a little man in a light-coloured raincoat and cap. He had a colourless and expressionless face, slightly inflamed eyelids, pale eyes – the sort of face you immediately forget.

'Is that you, Enno?' she exclaimed, and right away gripped her keys more tightly in her hand. 'What are you doing here? I've got
15 no money and nothing to eat, and I'm not letting you into the flat either.'

The little man made a dismissive gesture. 'Don't get upset, Eva. Don't be cross with me. I just wanted to say hello. Hello, Eva. There you are!'

20 'Hello Enno,' she said, reluctantly, having known her husband for many years. She waited a while, and then laughed briefly and sardonically. 'All right, we've said hello as you wanted, so why don't you go? But it seems you're not going, so what have you really come for?'

25 'See here, Evie,' he said. 'You're a sensible woman, you're someone a man can talk to…' He embarked on a long and

involved account of how he could no longer extend his sick leave, because he had been off for twenty-six weeks. He had to go back to work, otherwise they would pack him off back to the army, which
30 had allowed him to go to the factory in the first place because he was a precision toolmaker and those were in short supply. 'You see, the thing is,' he concluded his account, 'that I have to have a fixed address for the next few days. And so I thought…'

She shook her head emphatically. She was so tired she could drop,
35 and she was longing to be back in her flat, where much more work was waiting for her. But she wasn't going to let him in, not if she had to stand outside half the night.

Quickly he added, in a tone that immediately struck her as insincere, 'Don't say no, Evie, I haven't finished yet. I swear I want nothing from
40 you, no money, no food, nothing. Just let me bed down on the sofa. No need for any sheets. I don't want to be the least trouble to you.'

Again, she shook her head. If only he would stop talking; he really ought to know she didn't believe a word of it. He had never kept a promise in his life.

45 She asked, 'Why don't you get one of your girlfriends to put you up? They usually come through for something like this!'

He shook his head. 'No, Evie, I'm through with women, I can't deal with them any more, I want no more of them. If I think about it, you were always the best of them anyway, you know that. We had some
50 good years back then, you know, when the kids were small.'

In spite of herself, her face lit up at the recollection of their early married years. They really had been good years, when he was working as a machinist, taking home sixty marks a week, before he turned work shy.

55 Immediately Enno Kluge saw the chink. 'You see, Evie, you see, you still have a bit of a soft spot for me, and that's why you'll let me sleep on the sofa.' […]

She didn't say a word, and he went on, because it was his belief that you could talk your way into or out of anything and that if you were
60 persistent enough, in the end people would just give in. […]

She spoke at last: 'Look, Enno, I don't care if you stay here till midnight talking, I'm not taking you back. I'm never doing that again; I don't care what you say or what you do. I'm not going to let you wreck everything again with your laziness and your horses and your
65 hussies. You've done it three times, and then a fourth, and then more, but I've reached my limit, and that's it. I'm going to sit down on the steps, because I'm tired, I've been on my feet since six. If you want to, you can sit down, I don't care. You can talk or not, that's up to you: as I said, I don't care. But you're not setting foot in my apartment
70 ever again!'

Now look at the marking advice to the examiner that is listed below:

'In this passage the writer encourages the reader to feel dislike towards Enno Kluge.'

To what extent do you agree with this view?

You should write about:

- your own impressions of Enno as he is presented here
- how the writer has created these impressions. **[10]**

Give:

- **0 marks** for responses where there is nothing worthy of credit.

- **1–2 marks** to those who express simple personal opinion linked to basic textual support, for example, *I don't like Enno because he seems like a bad husband.*

- **3–4 marks** to those who give a personal opinion supported by straightforward textual references. These responses will show limited interaction with the text, for example, *I don't like Enno because he has treated his wife badly 'with your laziness and your horses and your hussies'.*

- **5–6 marks** to those who give an evaluation of the text and its effects, supported by appropriate textual references. These responses will show some critical awareness of the text, for example, *We are encouraged to dislike Enno because he is presented as having been a poor husband in the past with his 'laziness', his 'horses' and his 'hussies'.*

- **7–8 marks** to those who give a critical evaluation of the text and its effects, supported by well-selected textual references. They will show clear engagement with the text, for example, *The writer encourages us to dislike Enno because he is presented as having been a poor husband who has wrecked 'everything' in the past with his 'laziness', his gambling ('horses') and his other women ('hussies'). The list of evidence against him encourages the reader to feel the same distrust of him that his wife does.*

- **9–10 marks** to those who give a persuasive evaluation of the text and its effects, supported by convincing, well-selected examples and purposeful textual references. These responses will show engagement and involvement, where students take an overview to make accurate and perceptive comments on the text, for example, *The writer presents a clear comparison between the hard-working and downtrodden Eva Kluge and her opportunistic ex-husband. Our sympathies lie with her and as such her distrust of Enno becomes our distrust, established because he has wrecked 'everything' with his 'laziness', gambling and other women on numerous occasions in the past ('three times', 'then a fourth' and 'then more').*

These mark bands break down the mark allowances to explain the types of skills you need to show to gain those marks. You need to show these skills using a few points, however (not just the one used in the example). The list of 'areas for possible evaluation' gives you an idea of the type of points you might draw upon. There may be other points worthy of consideration too.

Areas for possible evaluation:

- Presentation of Eva in comparison to the way Enno is presented – at beginning and end of extract

- Physical description of Enno – 'colourless and expressionless face', 'slightly inflamed eyelids', 'pale eyes', 'the sort of face you immediately forget'

- Eva's initial reaction – 'gripped her keys more tightly', assumes he wants something: 'I've got no money and nothing to eat.'

- Sense of his dishonesty – 'I just wanted to say hello.'

- Sense that Eva has been here before – 'what have you really come here for?'

- He is persuasive – used to telling stories: 'long and involved account', uses flattery: 'you were always the best of them'

- 'Insincere'/'she didn't believe a word of it'/'He had never kept a promise in his life'

- Arrogant – he expects her to give in: 'if you were persistent enough' then 'people would just give in'

- List of the ways he failed as a husband – 'laziness', 'horses', 'hussies' – 'three times', 'then a fourth', 'then more'

Activity 4

Divide into pairs. Using the mark scheme opposite, try to mark your partner's response to Activity 3. If you think some of their work is worthy of a mark in the 7–8 band but elsewhere their comments are only good enough for the 3–4 band, you will probably end up giving a mark of 5 or 6 to reflect this.

Activity 5

When you have given your partner's response a mark out of 10, choose one area that you think you could improve upon. Rewrite that part of their answer to demonstrate how you would do this.

Activity 6

Now read the question and extract below:

> How do you react to the character of Fermín Romero de Torres in these lines? **[10]**

Extract from *The Shadow of the Wind* by Carlos Ruiz Zafón

The following extract is narrated by Daniel, who is a young man who works in his father's bookshop. Daniel was recently helped by the beggar Fermín Romero de Torres after he had been beaten up and left in the street by an attacker.

Business in the bookshop was picking up, and my father and I had more on our hands than we could juggle. 'At this rate we'll have to hire another person to help us find the orders,' my father remarked. 'What we
5 really need is someone very special, half detective, half poet, someone who won't charge much or be afraid to tackle the impossible.'

'I think I have the right candidate,' I said.

I found Fermín Romero de Torres in his usual lodgings
10 below the arches of Calle Fernando. The beggar was putting together the front page of the Monday paper from bits he had rescued from a waste bin. […]

'Good morning,' I said quietly. 'Do you remember me?'

The beggar raised his head, and a wonderful smile
15 suddenly lit up his face.

'Do mine eyes deceive me? How are things with you, my friend? You'll accept a swig of red wine, I hope?'

'It's on me today,' I said. 'Are you hungry?'

'Well, I wouldn't say no to a good plate of seafood,
20 but I'll eat anything that's thrown at me.'

On our way to the bookshop, Fermín Romero de Torres filled me in on all manner of escapades he had devised during the last weeks to avoid the Security Services, and in particular one Inspector Fumero, his
25 nemesis, with whom he appeared to have a running battle.

'Fumero?' I asked. That was the name of the soldier who murdered Clara Barceló's father in Montjuïc Castle at the outbreak of the war.

30 The little man nodded fearfully, turning pale. He looked famished and dirty, and he stank from months of living on the streets. The poor fellow had no idea where I was taking him, and I noticed a certain apprehension, a growing anxiety that he tried to hide with incessant
35 chatter. When we arrived at the shop, he gave me a troubled look.

'Please come in. This is my father's bookshop. I'd like to introduce you to him.'

The beggar hunched himself up, a bundle of grime
40 and nerves. 'No, no, I wouldn't hear of it. I don't look presentable, and this is a classy establishment. I would embarrass you…'

My father put his head around the door, glanced at the beggar, and then looked at me out of the corner of his
45 eye.

'Dad, this is Fermín Romero de Torres.'

'At your service,' said the beggar, almost shaking.

My father smiled at him calmly and stretched out his hand. The beggar didn't dare take it, mortified by his
50 appearance and the filth that covered his skin.

'Listen, I think it's best if I go away and leave you,' he stammered.

My father took him gently by the arm. 'Not at all, my son has told me you're going to have lunch with us.'

55 The beggar looked at us amazed, terrified.

'Why don't you come up to our home and have a nice hot bath?' said my father. 'Afterwards, if that's all right, we could walk down to Can Solé for lunch.'

Activity 7

The answers on pages 51–52 are in response to the question in Activity 6. Read them carefully and see if you can put them in rank order.

Student 1

I react to the character of Fermín Romero by feeling sorry for him. He is a beggar and has to take bits of the newspaper out of the bin in order to read it. I think he is excited to see Daniel because he thinks he will have food for him. He is really pleased that Daniel has brought him some wine: 'You'll accept a swig of red wine, I hope?' I am glad that someone is looking after him but I am not convinced that taking him alcohol is the answer. He is a criminal and has been in trouble with the police. This might have been because he was drunk. It would be better for Daniel to take him for dinner like he suggests instead of giving him wine. I suppose he must be desperate because he is a beggar: 'I'll eat anything that's thrown at me'. I think he is embarrassed because he smells and does not want to go into the bookshop. I feel sorry for him because it must be horrible to feel like that.

Student 2

Fermín Romero de Torres is presented as quite a character and even before we meet him it is clear that the reader will like him. Daniel thinks he is the 'right candidate' to fill his father's requirements of 'someone very special' who is 'half detective' and 'half poet'. This, and the fact that Daniel thinks he won't be 'afraid to tackle the impossible', sets him up as an intriguing and exciting character. Although Fermín is described as 'the beggar' there is no sense that he is downtrodden or pathetic, as we might expect; instead we know that on being spoken to 'he raised his head' and his face was 'lit up' by a 'wonderful smile'. He is warm in response to Daniel, calling him 'my friend' and generously offering him 'a swig of red wine'. My impressions of him are immediately favourable. It is clear that he is a humorous and lively character as he fills Daniel in 'on all manner of escapades', making him seem an entertaining storyteller as well as accomplished in avoiding the 'Security Services'. The use of the word 'escapade' makes it sound like his life is filled with adventure. His fear of Inspector Fumero is clear, though: he turns 'pale' at the mention of his name and at this point Daniel confirms that in his appearance he is the 'famished and dirty' looking beggar we might expect, generating sympathy and concern. Although he is in a bad state it is clear that he has pride and is alarmed at the thought of meeting Daniel's father, as he is 'mortified by his appearance' and the 'filth that covered his skin'. We see a change in the lively and talkative nature as he stammers and is keen to leave them. I get the sense that he is not used to people treating him kindly or with respect and he does not know how to respond.

Student 3

My reaction to Fermín is that he is presented as quite happy: 'raised his head, and a wonderful smile suddenly lit up his face'. He is a beggar and I feel sorry for him but I am pleased that Daniel is giving him some food: 'It's on me today.' I am alarmed that he has a 'running battle' with an Inspector. When he nods 'fearfully, turning pale' I am worried for him and think he must be scared. I think he needs a break and someone to take care of him: 'he looked famished and dirty', and I am a bit sad that he is feeling 'a growing anxiety' about where Daniel is taking him. It must be hard for him to trust people. It is also sad that he feels embarrassed in front of Daniel's father: 'mortified by his appearance and the filth that covered his skin'. I am happy that they are going to feed him: 'you're going to have lunch with us', and that they will clean him up: 'Why don't you come up to our home and have a nice hot bath?'

Activity 8

Below are some examiner comments which accompanied the answers on pages 51–52.

1. First of all, match the right examiner commentary to each answer.

2. When you have done that, try to complete the task which accompanies each of the comments.

Examiner A

Here the student tracks through the text and links a number of valid points with appropriate evidence selections. The answer lacks explanation of the reactions and how the text creates them.

a) Take three point/evidence combinations from the answer that Examiner A describes and improve them.

Examiner B

This student gives one or two valid reactions: they feel sorry for him and recognize Fermín's embarrassment, but there is also some misreading.

b) Explain what the student misread and what the text actually revealed.

Examiner C

This is a very thorough and detailed answer.

c) Select three points that this student makes well and explain why they are made well.

COMPONENT 1

Section B Writing

Introduction to Component 1, Section B Writing

Component 1 at a glance

Component 1	Section B Writing
• 40% of total marks for GCSE English Language • Assessment length: 1 hour 45 minutes • Section A Reading • Section B Writing	• 20% of total grade • Complete ONE creative writing task taken from four titles. • Spend 45 minutes on this task, including planning and proofreading.

What types of tasks will be in Section B Writing?

In Section B of the Component 1 exam you will be given four titles for a piece of creative prose writing. You must read ALL titles very carefully and then choose ONE title for your own writing. It is crucial that you select your title carefully to make sure that you can produce a piece of sustained writing and that you are able to write in an engaging and coherent manner.

You are expected to produce a piece of prose writing approximately 450–600 words in length for this section. Although you may choose to include descriptions of events, places or people to enhance your writing, this is not a piece of descriptive writing.

What is covered in this chapter?

This chapter will help you to prepare for the Writing section of the Component 1 exam. You will have the opportunity to think about the following:

- how to plan your prose writing
- how to develop your writing
- how to conclude or end a piece of writing
- ways to interest your reader
- how to use language imaginatively and creatively
- how to proofread your work.

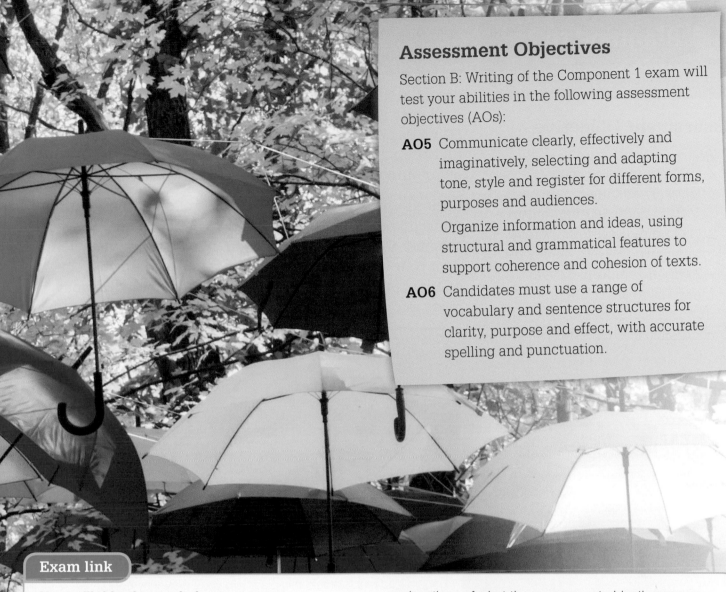

Assessment Objectives

Section B: Writing of the Component 1 exam will test your abilities in the following assessment objectives (AOs):

AO5 Communicate clearly, effectively and imaginatively, selecting and adapting tone, style and register for different forms, purposes and audiences.

Organize information and ideas, using structural and grammatical features to support coherence and cohesion of texts.

AO6 Candidates must use a range of vocabulary and sentence structures for clarity, purpose and effect, with accurate spelling and punctuation.

Exam link

How will this chapter help me prepare for the exam?

Each unit of this chapter will guide you through a range of different skills and techniques that you will find useful for the exam. There will be plenty of opportunities to work through different activity types, which will help you to decide how to choose the best title to work with when faced with a choice in the exam. There will also be the chance to think about a range of different ideas for your writing. For example, there are a variety of possible approaches that can be taken in creative writing and this chapter will encourage you to try them out, and analyse sample student responses which have used them too.

To help you understand how you are being assessed in the exam there will also be opportunities for you to read and assess different writing styles. There will be further explanations of what the assessment objectives mean and what you need to do to fulfil these. Narrative writing will be broken down into sections to encourage you to think about the component sections of your writing and how you can make each of these more effective.

There are opportunities for you to produce writing of your own and to assess your own work or that of a classmate. You can revise for the Writing section of the exam by completing the activities in this chapter and then by completing sample exam tasks in timed conditions. Always revisit your work: proofread it carefully but also think about how you can improve specific examples of vocabulary and the way you develop the plot/characters/tension, in addition to checking and refining your technical accuracy.

Good luck and enjoy writing!

1 Planning to write

Assessment Objective

- **AO5**
  – 1 Communicate clearly, effectively and imaginatively, selecting and adapting tone, style and register for different forms, purposes and audiences.
  – 2 Organize information and ideas, using structural and grammatical features to support coherence and cohesion of texts.

In the Component 1 Writing exam you will be given a choice of four titles, from which you select ONE to write about. Your writing will be a piece of creative prose – this means a long piece of fictional writing. Before you start writing it is essential that you pause and think carefully about what you will write and how you will organize or develop your work. Many students begin to write with no real sense of direction and often find that they lose focus in their work or they run out of things to write.

Some students like to produce a brief plan for their writing while others simply spend one or two minutes pulling together their ideas in their head. It is up to you how you plan your work but it is vital that you give yourself a couple of minutes to reflect on the titles and then organize your ideas into a sequence.

In the exam you will see a list of four titles. For example:

EITHER (a) A tough day.

OR (b) It was beautiful.

OR (c) Write about a time when you were at a Christmas party.

OR (d) Write a story which begins: 'If only I could go back in time…' **[40]**

Activity 1

Look at the plan below. Could you write a narrative based on this generalized plan? Would this plan help you? Why/why not?

Set the scene	Describe first character	Develop the detail	Introduce problem	Ending

Activity 2

This student's plan is far more specific.

Army basic training country race – describe the people, instructor, location, etc.	→	Main character feels intimidated by other competitors	→	Introduce another character – bigheaded, mocking the others	→	Introduce complication – have to cross a substantial stream – chaos ensues	→	Bedraggled, wet and very much a team, they cross the finish line

1. Look at the information in the plan and see if you can add some additional annotations to further develop the characters, storyline and action.

2. Using this type of plan, choose one of the four titles above and plan your own sequence of events.

Activity 3

Now look at your own plan from Activity 2 and see if you can answer the following questions to assess how much thought you have put into what you are going to write.

1. How will your story fit the title?
2. Will your narrative be written in the first person or third person?
3. Where will the action begin?
4. Which people will feature in your narrative?
5. Are you going to include any specific descriptive details?
6. What is going to happen to the main character?
7. How will you build the information towards the final paragraph?
8. How will your narrative end?

Tip Choose a title that you feel will allow you to write in detail but that will also allow you to write in a style that suits you. For example, do you prefer to write about events based on your own experiences or do you prefer to write imaginatively?

Activity 4

Look at the short story below. This story has been written in 128 words, which would be far too brief in the exam, which suggests 450–600 words.

1. Read the story carefully. As a reader, what else do you want to know?
2. Discuss in pairs how you could develop and improve it.

'The Long Walk Home' by Paul Mark Tag

Tuesday's shadows lengthened in Lahaina, on the Island of Maui. Pristine air made the neighboring islands of Lanai and Molokai appear ever so close.

5 Alice waited patiently under the banyan tree for her husband, returning from his day of fishing. As the sun set she spotted him beyond the distant reach of the massive tree. They engaged in small talk as they trudged up the narrow streets.

As home drew near, Alice spotted a younger woman
10 ahead.

'Hello, Mom — how are you?'

Alice stared at the woman briefly, but then continued walking.

'Come on Harry. Let's get you inside and fed.'

15 The daughter's face saddened. It had been more than a year now — since Alice forgot that Harry had died at sea, on a Tuesday, ten years earlier.

2 The first paragraph

Assessment Objectives

- **AO5**
  – 1 Communicate clearly, effectively and imaginatively, selecting and adapting tone, style and register for different forms, purposes and audiences.
  – 2 Organize information and ideas, using structural and grammatical features to support coherence and cohesion of texts.

- **AO6**
  – Candidates must use a range of vocabulary and sentence structures for clarity, purpose and effect, with accurate spelling and punctuation.

Starting a piece of narrative writing can be difficult. Writers know that they have to make an impact and 'hook' their readers, but producing something that achieves this is more difficult than it sounds. Pay close attention to the openings of any books you read or films you watch and see if you can pick up any tips for your writing.

An effective first paragraph will:

- captivate the reader's mind (get them thinking)
- promise good things to come
- be clever, witty or humorous but not too complex.

Activity 1

The following are a selection of different ways you could begin a piece of narrative writing. Match each approach with a correct definition.

> Tell a brief story.   Set an interesting scene.
>
> Use a definitive statement.   Give a problem.
>
> Pose a question.   Dismiss a common view.

A Introducing a story in this way can capture a reader's attention as they will be keen to see if the problem can be resolved.

B A definitive statement gives your stance on an issue. You can then follow the statement with interesting and/or factual information to provoke the reader.

C Start with an anecdote or background details to grab the reader's attention. Be sure the information makes it clear that the story will come after it.

D State something that most people will agree with and set about producing a narrative in which you take a different or opposing view.

E A powerful description can grab the reader's attention. The reader will be intrigued by the setting and wonder what happened there and why it is significant.

F This style of opening works well if the question is relevant throughout the narrative. The question should be answered at some point before the end.

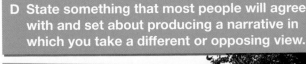

Activity 2

In small groups, work through each of the different ways of beginning a story suggested in Activity 1. Write down four or five lines that you could use for each style of introduction. Share your ideas with the class. Try to be imaginative without becoming too far-fetched. Remember, these approaches are just some suggestions – there are many other ways to begin a story and if you have a good idea in the exam, use it.

You cannot plan in advance what you will write in the exam. You can only practise your writing skills and be ready to apply them in different ways. The way you begin your writing will depend on the titles you are given in the exam, and how you choose to express your ideas on that particular day. Some students like to begin their narrative with an action scene or a clear description of where the narrative is being set. The following activity will help you to write an action scene. You can use the skills you develop in different types of writing.

Activity 3

Prepositions are words that tell you about timing, position or direction. Prepositions are often used in narrative writing to give a precise indication of where the action is happening.

1. The following are prepositions. Can you think of any others?

between   **behind**   **opposite**   **through**   **under**   **towards**   **across**

Now, imagine you are narrating an action story where there is chaos and commotion in a street.

2. The following lists will give you some words to enhance your writing. Can you add any others?

Words to describe the street:
panic, pandemonium, uproar, horror, hysteria, terror, frenzy, madness, mayhem

Words that will give the author's opinion:
unimaginable, inconceivable, alarming, terrifying, horrifying, chaotic, dreadful

Verbs to describe action:
swarming, scrambling, jostling, racing, escaping, fleeing, dodging, ducking

Adverbs to describe the motion:
frantically, frenetically, frenziedly, furiously, wildly

 Tip Think about describing how people react – this will help you to suggest a real sense of action and urgency.

3. Write an introductory paragraph to an action story where there is chaos and commotion in the street. If you are still struggling, you might like to think about the following:

    *   people   *   buildings   *   movements   *   cars

(3) Developing the narrative

Assessment Objectives

- **AO5**

  – 1 Communicate clearly, effectively and imaginatively, selecting and adapting tone, style and register for different forms, purposes and audiences.

  – 2 Organize information and ideas, using structural and grammatical features to support coherence and cohesion of texts.

- **AO6**

  – Candidates must use a range of vocabulary and sentence structures for clarity, purpose and effect, with accurate spelling and punctuation.

In the exam you will have approximately 45 minutes to plan, write and proofread your narrative. Getting your timing right when writing a story is important. It is also important that you finish your narrative but that you don't finish it too quickly and risk producing undeveloped and brief writing. Do not be too ambitious in terms of storyline as 45 minutes is not a huge amount of time. Focus instead on developing narratives that are convincing and engaging.

Activity 1

You have been asked to write an account of an embarrassing moment. Spend two or three minutes making a list in pairs about incidents that would be embarrassing. Remember: you do not have to tell the truth, but you should not write anything too absurd or unbelievable.

Activity 2

Choose one embarrassing moment from the list you have produced. Think carefully about where you will start and where you will finish your account. Try to write six sentences to summarize what will happen.

Tip The way you build up your narrative is vital. Your narrative style must engage your reader. The student who has written the plan below might use a style where they mock themselves over the silly things they do. This will encourage a reader to have sympathy for the main character, if they are able to laugh *with* the writer, rather than at them.

Activity 3

Look at the student's plan below. They have written a plan for their embarrassing story.

1. The timescale for the story is very brief. There is only one main character (and that could be you if you have written in the first person). What could this student do to make the narrative more interesting?

2. What type of person would write this type of story? What details do you think it is important to know about the person in the story?

- Too late for breakfast
- Bus journey to school
- Embarrassing dancing in front of pretty girl
- Growling rumbling tummy
- Sitting test in silence in English
- Stomach keeps growling
- Lunchtime, hurrying to table and tip food all over someone

Activity 4

Read the first three paragraphs from a sample student response below.

The student has written 167 words without getting round to the actual story. However, the details they give build up a sense of character and establish the tone for the story to come.

1. Copy out the answer and annotate it by underlining any phrases that you find amusing.

2. Underline any phrases that you feel are effectively punctuated.

3. To continue the narrative the student plans to describe some hungry grumbling stomach noises in a quiet class. Bullet point five or six ideas of how they could introduce and develop this.

4. Take each of your bullet points and, using a thesaurus and dictionary, select a range of effective verbs (to describe the movement and actions that occur) that will help make your writing more interesting.

Little did I know it at the time... but as I woke up that morning I was about to have the worst day of my life...

Yes, I was too late up for my weety-pops, but other than my mother chasing me down the road in her dressing gown for a goodbye kiss, my morning had started well. Before boarding the bus, a few minor hiccups occurred such as when I slipped on a thin layer of ice which filled a hole (or crater to be precise) left by last year's floods! Then there was the girl (a pretty stunning sixth former) who saw me dancing to One Direction (honestly, I have no idea who put it on my iPod)...

However, I was used to this level of embarrassment. This was the usual stuff, pretty low level. I had once experienced medium level embarrassment but those days were gone (no more the days I wore brown y-fronts I had borrowed from my dad, on a PE day, because mine had 'run out').

Activity 5

With a partner look back at the list you made about embarrassing moments in Activity 1. Take one of these examples and together make a list of the feelings you would experience. Try to break down the feelings into tiny steps to build up tension.

Tip Roald Dahl is a master storyteller. The way he builds up tension is particularly effective. Try reading one of his stories (perhaps *Boy*) and see what you can learn from his style and use of language.

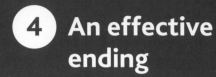

4 An effective ending

Assessment Objective

- **AO5**
  – 1 Communicate clearly, effectively and imaginatively, selecting and adapting tone, style and register for different forms, purposes and audiences.
  – 2 Organize information and ideas, using structural and grammatical features to support coherence and cohesion of texts.

There are many different ways that a writer can conclude a narrative. An effective ending can evoke a range of different reactions such as:

- sadness that the story is over or because a character is emotional
- relief that a series of events have finished
- shock that something unexpected has happened
- surprise – usually with a clever or circular ending
- horror when the ending is a complete disaster
- smugness – you had it worked out all along.

When you are writing, try to aim to have a dramatic impact at the end as this will leave your reader with one last thing to be impressed with.

Activity 1

Read the extracts on pages 62–63 which conclude three different stories.

1. Copy and complete the table below to help you explore each paragraph.

	Extract 1	Extract 2	Extract 3
What do you learn about the main character?			
Why do you think the action is set where it is?			
How does the main character feel?			
What do you think has happened to the main character?			
If you could ask one question about this book, what would it be?			

2. Which of these three stories would you like to read, and why?

Extract 1

Extract from *Dance of the Happy Shades* by Alice Munro

May heard his car start and then she ran out after him, as if she wanted to call something, as if she wanted to call 'Help' or 'Stay'. But she did not call anything, she stood with her mouth open in the dust in front of the gas pumps, and he would not have heard her anyway; he gave one wildly negative wave out of the window of his car and roared away to the north. 5

Extract 2

Extract from 'The Stolen Body' by H. G. Wells

He lay there for the space of about three hours before he was found.
And in spite of the pain and suffering of his wounds, and of the dim
damp place in which he lay; in spite of the tears – wrung from him by
his physical distress – his heart was full of gladness to know that he
5   was nevertheless back once more in the kindly world of men.

Extract 3

Extract from *The Hunt for Red October* by Tom Clancy

Ryan missed the dawn. He boarded a TWA 757 that left
Dulles on time, at 7:05am. The sky was overcast, and
when the aircraft burst through the cloud layer into sunlight,
Ryan did something he had never done before. For the first
5   time in his life, Jack Ryan fell asleep on an airplane.

Activity 2

Think back to the work you completed on developing a narrative about an embarrassing moment (pages 60–61). In order to maximize the effect you have on the reader, the timing of your ending is crucial.

1. Take the story you were planning from pages 60–61 and use the table below to sketch out some details that will help you when concluding your narrative. Think carefully about the final sentence for each option.

2. Now swap your work with a partner and ask them to write down any questions that they feel you need to address to make your ending more effective. Which ending do they prefer?

3. Select one option. Write one paragraph to conclude your story. Take time to think about the language you use and how you break down the information to have more impact on the reader.

In the middle of the embarrassment	Immediately after	Resolution – several hours later

Activity 3

Look at the following ending types. Write a brief definition for each type:

Circular ending   **Fairytale**

Resolution   **Cliffhanger**

Tip Remember, you have many options when you conclude your story. From the cliffhanger to the resolution, the most important thing is that you think about the reaction you want to leave your reader with and then write carefully to ensure your ending is both enjoyable and leaves a lasting impact.

(5) Writing a narrative

Assessment Objectives

- **AO5**
  – 1 Communicate clearly, effectively and imaginatively, selecting and adapting tone, style and register for different forms, purposes and audiences.
  – 2 Organize information and ideas, using structural and grammatical features to support coherence and cohesion of texts.
- **AO6**
  – Candidates must use a range of vocabulary and sentence structures for clarity, purpose and effect, with accurate spelling and punctuation.

Many students enjoy the Writing section of Component 1 as they have a chance to communicate something personal when they write. This is the only chance in your GCSE English Language exam that you have to really showcase your imaginative and creative skills. In this unit, you will plan and write a narrative, but you will also have the opportunity to explore some of the pitfalls of GCSE narrative writing.

Activity 1

Spend two minutes reading through the titles and tasks below and select one to write about.

EITHER

(a) Why did I have to open my big mouth?

OR (b) Showtime.

OR (c) Write about a time when you were tricked.

OR (d) Write a story which begins: 'I have never laughed so much in my life…' **[40]**

Activity 2

Take your chosen title or task and spend no longer than five minutes making a list or spider diagram of things you will include. Make a note of any words and phrases that come to mind that you could use in your writing.

Activity 3

1. Spend one or two minutes looking at your plan from Activity 2. Write down numbers to help you plan the sequence of events and to make sure your organization is effective.

2. Now you need to write your narrative. Spend around 35 minutes writing down your ideas. Remember to paragraph your work and think carefully about your sentence structure and the vocabulary you use.

Activity 4

Now look back through your story. Follow the proofreading tip on this page, reading one sentence at a time. You should also:

- Check the punctuation of your work.
- See if you can improve any vocabulary.
- Check that your work is paragraphed.
- Make sure your narrative makes sense.

Progress check

Now swap your work with a partner and ask them for honest feedback. What do they think of your characters? Do they think you need more detail/description? Do they understand everything? What do they think of the ending? Ask them to annotate your work in a different colour and then reflect on their comments.

Tip Proofreading is essential, especially if you are prone to making errors. When proofreading, put your finger on the punctuation at the end of a sentence and then read *just* that sentence to make sure it makes sense.

Tip There are many pitfalls when writing a narrative. Although some of the ideas below can be very successful, if they are written in a stereotypical manner they may be less engaging and original. Answers that are pre-prepared are often forced to fit a topic and are also usually less convincing.

- Overly personal narratives that include text language and inappropriate content are unlikely to gain high marks.
- Some students try to evoke the examiner's pity – it won't improve your mark if you give a sob story. You are only marked on the quality of what you produce.
- Although it is fine to base your narrative on something else, avoid a complete 'rip off' of a well-known film. Films usually last a couple of hours and you have very little time to produce an in-depth film-style narrative.
- Avoid anything that forces you to make your ideas fit a title.

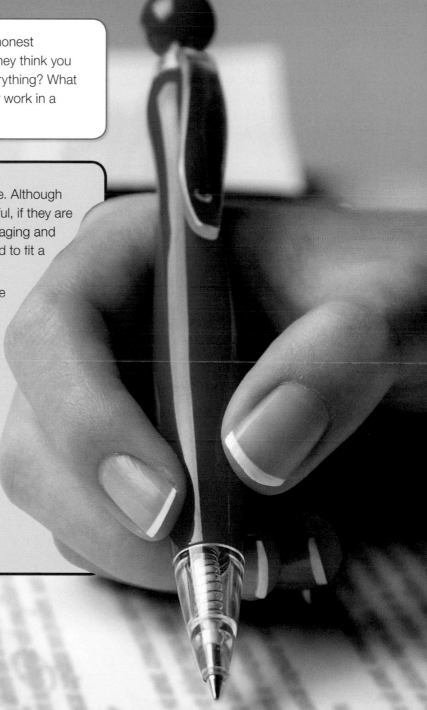

Assessment Criteria for Writing: Component 1, Section B

	AO5 Communication and organization *24 marks*	AO6 Vocabulary, sentence structure, spelling and punctuation *16 marks*
Band 5	**20–24 marks** • The writing is fully coherent and controlled (plot and characterization are developed with detail, originality and imagination). • The writing is clearly and imaginatively organized (narrative is sophisticated and fully engages the reader's interest). • Structure and grammatical features are used ambitiously to give the writing cohesion and coherence. • Communication is ambitious and consistently conveys precise meaning.	**14–16 marks** • There is appropriate and effective variation of sentence structures. • Virtually all sentence construction is controlled and accurate. • A range of punctuation is used confidently and accurately. • Virtually all spelling, including that of complex irregular words, is correct. • Control of tense and agreement is totally secure. • A wide range of appropriate, ambitious vocabulary is used to create effect or convey precise meaning.
Band 4	**15–19 marks** • The writing is clearly controlled and coherent (plot and characterization show convincing detail and some originality and imagination). • The writing is clearly organized (narrative is purposefully shaped and developed). • Structure and grammatical features are used accurately to support cohesion and coherence. • Communication shows some ambition and conveys precise meaning.	**11–13 marks** • Sentence structure is varied to achieve particular effects. • Control of sentence construction is secure. • A range of punctuation is used accurately. • Spelling, including that of irregular words, is secure. • Control of tense and agreement is secure. • Vocabulary is ambitious and used with precision.
Band 3	**10–14 marks** • The writing is mostly controlled and coherent (plot and characterization show some detail and development). • The writing is organized (narrative has shape and direction). • Structure and grammatical features are used with some accuracy to convey meaning. • Communication is clear but limited in ambition.	**7–10 marks** • There is variety in sentence structure. • Control of sentence construction is mostly secure. • A range of punctuation is used, mostly accurately. • Most spelling, including that of irregular words, is correct. • Control of tense and agreement is mostly secure. • Vocabulary is beginning to develop and is used with some precision.

	AO5 Communication and organization *24 marks*	AO6 Vocabulary, sentence structure, spelling and punctuation *16 marks*
Band 2	**5–9 marks** • There is some control and coherence (some control of plot and characterization). • There is some organization (narrative is beginning to have some shape and development). • Structure and grammatical features are used to convey meaning. • Communication is limited but clear.	**4–6 marks** • There is some variety of sentence structure. • There is some control of sentence construction. • There is some control of a range of punctuation. • The spelling is usually accurate. • Control of tense and agreement is generally secure. • There is some range of vocabulary.
Band 1	**1–4 marks** • There is basic control and coherence (a basic sense of plot and characterization). • There is basic organization (paragraphs may be used to show obvious divisions). • There is some use of structure and grammatical features to convey meaning. • Communication is limited but some meaning is conveyed.	**1–3 marks** • There is a limited range of sentence structure. • Control of sentence construction is limited. • There is some attempt to use punctuation. • Some spelling is accurate. • Control of tense and agreement is limited. • There is a limited range of vocabulary.
	0 marks • Nothing worthy of credit.	**0 marks** • Nothing worthy of credit.

COMPONENT 2

Section A Reading

Introduction to Component 2, Section A Reading

Component 2 at a glance

Component 2
- 60% of total marks for GCSE English Language
- Assessment length: 2 hours
- Section A Reading
- Section B Writing

Section A Reading
- 30% of total grade
- Short and long answer questions covering all Reading Assessment Objectives (AOs)
- 1 hour (10 minutes reading and 50 minutes answering questions)

What types of texts will I read in this exam?

Component 2 texts are all non-fiction. You will meet a variety of these types of texts in this chapter, such as newspaper articles, websites, letters, leaflets and literary non-fiction, such as travel writing. In the exam you will have two texts: one will be from the 19th century and the other will be from the 21st century. The texts will have a broad link to allow you to combine information about a topic and compare/contrast the way the texts present ideas and points of view.

What is covered in this chapter?

This chapter will help you to prepare for the Reading section of the Component 2 exam. Component 2 covers all of the reading skills which are assessed in GCSE English Language – Assessment Objectives 1–4.

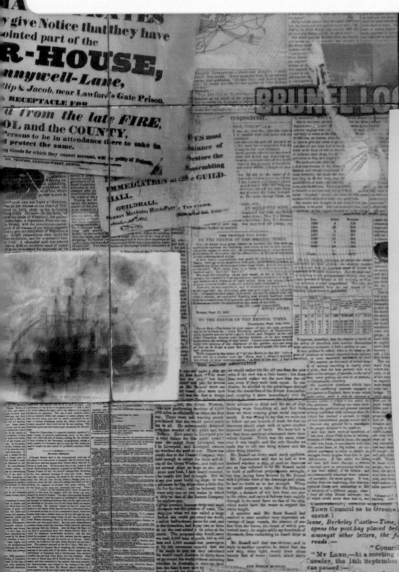

How will this chapter help me prepare for the exam?

Each unit of this chapter will guide you through one of the skills you will need to practise for the exam, such as inferring or evaluating. First, you will look at what the reading skill is and some of the ways it can be tested in the exam. There will be tips on how to do your best in the exam and sometimes advice about things to avoid. Often the texts used in this chapter are shorter than the ones you might face in the exam, which will help you develop your response to an exam-style question in a more focused way.

In order to help you understand how the skills are assessed, you will be taken through the requirements of each assessment objective. You will practise these skills on selected extracts and study examples of students' responses to exam-style questions. At the end of each unit, you will then practise an exam-style question to give you an idea of what it is like to answer a question in the exam.

There are plenty of opportunities throughout each unit for you to assess your own work and that of a classmate. Setting targets for improvement is part of an important process of 'plan–do–review', which will help you build on your strengths and tackle your weaknesses before the exam. Always take the opportunity to revisit your work in the light of the targets you have set. It is as valuable to improve a piece of work as to complete a new one.

Good luck!

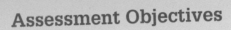

Assessment Objectives

Section A: Reading of the Component 2 exam will test your abilities in the following assessment objectives (AOs):

AO1 Identify and interpret explicit and implicit information and ideas.

Select and synthesize evidence from different texts.

AO2 Explain, comment on and analyse how writers use language and structure to achieve effects and influence readers, using relevant subject terminology to support their views.

AO3 Compare writers' ideas and perspectives, as well as how these are conveyed, across two or more texts.

AO4 Evaluate texts critically and support this with appropriate textual references.

1 Identifying explicit information and ideas

A key reading skill is choosing particular information and ideas in order to answer a question. Questions asking you to select **explicit** ideas might ask for a certain number of ideas: 'List three reasons why…' or 'List five things the writer says about…', or they may require an answer to a specific closed question: 'Who does the writer say is…?' or 'How much…?' or 'Where is…?'

Assessment Objective

● **AO1**
  – 1a Identify explicit information.
  – 1b Identify explicit ideas.

To tackle these types of questions you will need to identify the key words in the question and **scan** through the text to find them. You might also be guided in where to look for the information, with instructions such as 're-read the first paragraph…'. This tells you where to find the answer so you must only search there or you will not get the correct answer. The activities here will help you practise scanning for explicit information from an advert and shaping your response so it answers the question clearly.

Key terms

Explicit: stating something openly and directly
Scan: to glance through a text to find a key word or piece of information

Activity 1

The questions below all ask for specific information from a certain place. First, identify where to search and the key words in each question. Next, use the key words to scan for the answers.

> To answer these questions read the first paragraph of 'Discover the Northern Lights'.
>
> **a)** Where does a Hurtigruten voyage sail? [1]
>
> **b)** What is said to be the response of those who witness the Aurora Borealis? [1]
>
> **c)** What colours are the lights of the Aurora Borealis? [1]

Discover the Northern Lights

There is no better way to experience the Northern Lights than on a Hurtigruten voyage, sailing through sheltered coastal waters free from artificial light. The Aurora Borealis mesmerises all who will witness them, as this natural phenomenon produces a fascinating range of light from blue to green and white tinges, creating a wonderful backdrop to the spectacular coastal landscapes. With Hurtigruten's unrivalled knowledge and experience in navigating the region they will take you to the best areas for viewing this natural wonder.

A Hurtigruten voyage provides the perfect solution for seasoned cruisers and first timers alike who are searching for an intimate informal destination experience.

On board your ship you will enjoy the relaxed ambience with other like-minded travellers. Enjoy full board en-suite accommodation and sublime cuisine including three-course evening meals, which take advantage of the delicious local produce. Relax and enjoy the stunning scenery pass by from the plentiful outside deck space or enjoy the peace and tranquillity from the panorama lounge.

Activity 2

The four examples below answer question b) from Activity 1.
Discuss which two are clear enough to get the mark and why.

1 'The Aurora Borealis mesmerises all who will witness them.'

2 People who witness the Aurora Borealis are said to be 'mesmerised'.

3 Mesmerises.

4 They are mesmerised.

In example 3 above, the student finds the correct word to describe a person's response. However, just copying this single word as it appears in the text, 'mesmerises', says only what the lights do to a person, not what the response of the person is. A person can *be* mesmeris*ed*, not mesmeris*es*. Similarly, in example 1, writing out the quotation from the text puts the focus on what the Northern Lights do, whereas the question is angled on the *people*. Examples 2 and 4 would therefore gain the mark.

 Tip Word or angle your response carefully so that it answers the question.

Activity 3

Check over your own answers from Activity 1 to make sure they are focused on the question. For example, check you have listed all three colours for question c) and the word 'tinges'.

Activity 4

Now practise your scanning skills to find information for two questions which are focused, or angled, slightly differently. Discuss the focus of each question with a partner so you know what ideas/key words to scan for.

a) List three things you can enjoy on a Hurtigruten cruise. **[3]**
b) List three reasons to choose a Hurtigruten voyage. **[3]**

Some information is useful for both questions but some is only relevant for one. Remember to word your response to focus on the words/angle of the question.

2 Interpreting implicit information and ideas

Assessment Objective

- **AO1**
  - 1c Interpret implicit information.
  - 1d Interpret implicit ideas.

Implicit ideas can be hidden in a text, so to answer questions testing this reading skill you need to think like a detective finding clues. This involves thinking about the text carefully to explain and **interpret** what you read. These exam questions might be worded 'What does the writer mean when they say…?' or 'What does the writer suggest…?' As with finding explicit information, scanning through the text to find the words in the question might help, but you must also read between the lines to find the ideas and information that link to the question. The text and activities below will support you in using these skills.

Key terms

Implicit: meaning that is suggested but not directly expressed

Interpret: to explain the meaning of something

Activity 1

Identify the key topic word of this question. Then try to find the word in the extract from the newspaper article that follows.

> Explain what made Fraser's 17-day ordeal lost in the Australian bush dangerous. **[4]**

A woman missing in the Queensland rainforest in Australia for 17 days has been found alive

A woman missing for more than two weeks in a rugged Australian rainforest has stumbled out alive after surviving a chase by a crocodile and eating small fish, officials and reports said Thursday.

Shannon Fraser, 30, went missing on September 21 near the remote Josephine Falls in Queensland state after becoming disorientated, wearing just leggings, a shirt and flip flops.

She was spotted by a banana farmer on Wednesday, covered in cuts, welts, bruises and insect bites, the *Brisbane Courier-Mail* reported.

'She's lost lots of weight, she's covered in cuts and scratches, but she's in good spirits,' her brother Dylan Fraser told the newspaper.

Reports said she lost nearly 17 kilogrammes (37 pounds) during her ordeal.

The *Courier-Mail* said Fraser told her family that during her feat of survival she came face-to-face with a giant cassowary* flightless bird, and got chased by a two-metre (6.5-foot) freshwater crocodile.

*cassowary – bird which can grow to over 2m tall, weigh 45kg, run at 30mph with a long sharp spike on its inner toe; can deliver a powerful kick if harassed

Activity 2

The key word in the question, 'dangerous', does not appear in the text at all. But the whole of the text does show the dangers that Shannon Fraser faced. To answer the question in Activity 1 you first need to track through the text carefully and find all of the things that make this experience dangerous. Use your finger as a guide to follow the lines and stop whenever you get to a danger. If this were your exam text, you might well ring or highlight the relevant things you find. For this activity you can make a numbered list.

1. How many dangers can you find?
2. Check your answers with a partner. Did they find any dangers you missed?

Activity 3

So far you have identified information which might have answered a question such as 'List things which made Fraser's ordeal dangerous'. The question in Activity 1 uses the skills word *explain*, so you must give a reason why each of the things was a danger to Fraser's life. For example:

> Fraser was missing 'for 17 days' therefore she was alone in the Australian bush for a long time, and without food or water the length of time she was missing probably increased her chance of death.

Now answer the question in Activity 1 in full, using the following pointers:

- Look carefully at your list of dangers before you write to avoid saying the same or a similar thing twice. For example, the crocodile is mentioned at the beginning and the end of the article but you could comment on this and the cassowary by saying: 'One of the dangers she faces are the animals such as...'

- Think carefully about why each of the items you selected poses a danger to Fraser. Is it a danger to her physical health? Her mental well-being? Her whole life?

- Explain your ideas carefully using words such as 'because', 'so', 'therefore', 'which shows', 'which suggests', 'which implies'.

- Use synonyms for 'danger' to make your answer less repetitive: 'threat to her life', 'poses a hazard', 'puts her at great risk', 'she is in peril'.

Tip Remember that the value of a question tells you how long you should spend on it and how much you should write. In this question, grouping together similar examples of the same thing – like commenting on the crocodile and the cassowary together as two dangerous animals – would help you to avoid repeating ideas which have the same explanation. Therefore you can explain points about different ideas and pick up more marks.

3 Looking at explicit and implicit information together

In the Component 2 exam you will be asked questions about one text written in the 19th century. You need to use the skills you have learned about locating and explaining explicit and implicit information to tackle these texts. Use the activities in this unit to help you practise these skills on a letter written in 1853. It explains the work of a charity organization called a 'Ragged School', set up to provide free education to poor children in the 1800s. Read the letter and the exam questions which accompany it.

Assessment Objective

- **AO1**
  – 1 Identify and interpret explicit and implicit information and ideas.

Now, Ragged Schools have been set on foot by kind and Christian people on purpose to do good to these unhappy children. They are brought to these schools, and there they have their torn, dirty clothes taken off, and after being washed, and made nice and clean, they have others put on to wear all day, but at night they are obliged to have their dirty ones put on again, because their parents are so wicked, that if they went home in good clothes they would take them from them and sell them, and spend the money on something to drink. Then they would send the children out again in miserable and filthy rags, or nearly without clothes at all; so the kind people at the schools take care of the clean clothing for them at night. The children stay at school all day and have food provided for them. Sometimes they have one thing, sometimes another. The day I was at Dr Guthrie's school, they had each a basin of nice hot soup and a good-sized piece of bread. What a treat for these poor, neglected, hungry things!

1. List two words that are used to describe the people who run the Ragged Schools. **[1]**

2. Name four things the Ragged Schools do to help the 'unhappy children'. **[4]**

3. List three impressions you get of the parents of the children and support each with a quotation from the text. **[3]**

4. List three impressions you get of the children and support each with a quotation from the text. **[3]**

Activity 1

1. Which questions about the extract opposite are asking you to find explicit information from the text. Which questions about the extract want you to find and interpret implicit ideas? How do you know?

2. List strategies and tips you know about which will help you answer the questions on page 74. Share your ideas with a partner.

Activity 2

Answer the questions which accompany the letter. Follow the tips you thought about in Activity 1.

Activity 3

Look carefully again at the text and the suggested mark scheme below to decide how many marks you would have achieved for your answers to the questions opposite.

Question 1	Award 1 mark for both words, 0 marks for nothing or one word.
Question 2	Award 1 mark for each valid thing the school does to help.
Questions 3 and 4	Award 1 mark for each valid inference supported by a quotation, up to a maximum of 3.

Progress check

Assess your success:

- How many marks did you get? Did this surprise you? In what way?

- What strategies and tips did you use from Activity 1 which helped you answer the questions?

- Did you do better on the explicit or implicit questions, or was your achievement similar? You might like to look back at the activities on reading for explicit and implicit information and ideas on the previous pages to help you improve.

- What target might you set yourself or what do you need to remember to do in the exam?

4 Combining information from two texts

Assessment Objective

- **AO1**
  – 2 Select and synthesize evidence from different texts.

In the Component 2 exam you will have one 19th-century text and one from this century which will be linked in some way, possibly by their topic. At least one of the questions will want you to **synthesize** information from the two texts. This means that you must read both texts carefully, find and then combine the information required in your answer.

The texts in this unit both tell the legend of how a town in Snowdonia called Beddgelert got its name. Extract 1 is taken from a book called *Wild Wales* written by the English author George Borrow in 1862. Extract 2 is from the Beddgelert Tourism webpage.

Key term

Synthesize: to combine or put together

Tip Some of the words you read in a 19th-century text might be totally unfamiliar to you. Try to use the mood of the text and the activity or character being described as a clue to the meaning of the word. For 'paroxysm' you might put yourself in Llywelyn's shoes and deduce that the word could have something to do with his sudden emotions of pain and anger ('indignation') as he stabs ('transfixed') the dog with his spear.

Activity 1

Read Extract 1. Use the context of the extract and your own knowledge to work out the meanings of the following words:

a) besmeared

b) paroxysm

c) indignation

d) forthwith

e) transfixed

f) hastened

g) expired

Activity 2

Now read both texts and put together information on the three main characters in the story. Copy and complete the table below. Select more than one quotation for each character if possible to provide a range of details.

Character	Quotations from *Wild Wales* by George Borrow	Quotations from Beddgelert Tourism website
The wolf	'in quest of prey' 'the monster'	
The dog as the Prince returns from hunting/ his expedition		'the truant, stained and smeared with blood'
The feelings of the Prince as he finds out Gelert did not kill the baby		

Extract 1

Extract from *Wild Wales* by George Borrow

Llywelyn during his contests with the English had encamped with a few followers in the valley, and one day departed with his men on an expedition, leaving his infant son in a cradle in his tent, under 5 the care of his hound Gelert, after giving the child its fill of goat's milk. Whilst he was absent a wolf from the neighbouring mountains, in quest of prey, found its way into the tent, and was about to devour the child, when the watchful dog interfered, and after a 10 desperate conflict, in which the tent was torn down, succeeded in destroying the monster. Llywelyn returning at evening found the tent on the ground, and the dog, covered with blood, sitting beside it. Imagining that the blood with which Gelert was besmeared was that of his own son devoured by the 15 animal to whose care he had confided him, Llywelyn in a paroxysm of natural indignation forthwith transfixed the faithful creature with his spear. Scarcely, however, had he done so when his ears were startled by the cry of a child from beneath the fallen tent, and hastily 20 removing the canvas he found the child in its cradle, quite uninjured, and the body of an enormous wolf, frightfully torn and mangled, lying near. His breast was now filled with conflicting emotions, joy for the preservation of his son, and grief for the fate of his 25 dog, to whom he forthwith hastened. The poor animal was not quite dead, but presently expired, in the act of licking his master's hand. Llywelyn mourned over him as over a brother, buried him with funeral honours in the valley, and erected a tomb over him as over a 30 hero. From that time the valley was called Beth Gelert.

Extract 2

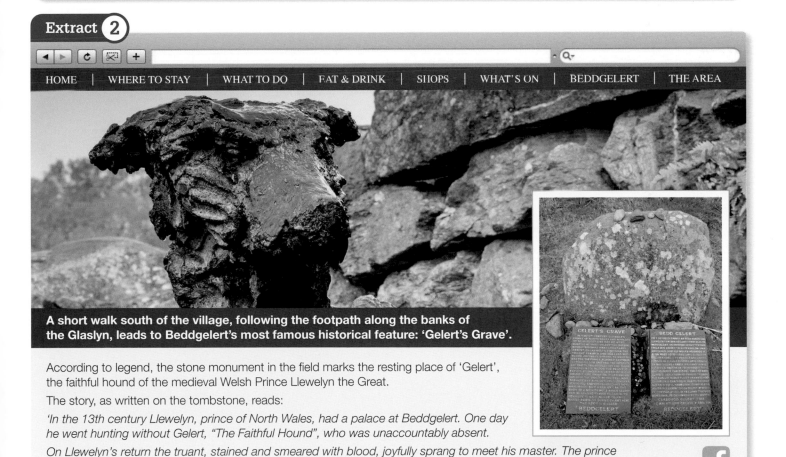

| HOME | WHERE TO STAY | WHAT TO DO | EAT & DRINK | SHOPS | WHAT'S ON | BEDDGELERT | THE AREA |

A short walk south of the village, following the footpath along the banks of the Glaslyn, leads to Beddgelert's most famous historical feature: 'Gelert's Grave'.

According to legend, the stone monument in the field marks the resting place of 'Gelert', the faithful hound of the medieval Welsh Prince Llewelyn the Great.

The story, as written on the tombstone, reads:

'In the 13th century Llewelyn, prince of North Wales, had a palace at Beddgelert. One day he went hunting without Gelert, "The Faithful Hound", who was unaccountably absent.

On Llewelyn's return the truant, stained and smeared with blood, joyfully sprang to meet his master. The prince alarmed hastened to find his son, and saw the infant's cot empty, the bedclothes and floor covered with blood.

The frantic father plunged his sword into the hound's side, thinking it had killed his heir. The dog's dying yell was answered by a child's cry.

Llewelyn searched and discovered his boy unharmed, but nearby lay the body of a mighty wolf which Gelert had slain. The prince filled with remorse is said never to have smiled again. He buried Gelert here.'

Activity 3

Look at the mark scheme below. You will notice that to achieve more than 1 mark for the exam-style question below you must provide a 'range' of detail from the text. There are no hard and fast rules about how many points are enough, but you need to show that you have considered enough of the ideas to show you understand the texts fully. Now tackle the exam question below:

> Explain what you learn about Gelert (the dog) in both texts. **[4]**

Remember:

- 'Relevant detail' means you must select points about the dog.
- Avoid repeating yourself if both texts say the same thing by using 'Both…'.
- Select quotations from both texts even if what you learn about the dog is the same.
- Say which text your ideas/quotations are from.
- Cover enough points from both texts to show a good understanding of the similarities and differences in what is said about the dog.

Mark	Criteria
0	• Nothing worthy of credit
1	• Some selection of relevant detail from both texts
2	• Selects a range of relevant detail from both texts
3	• Synthesizes with some understanding a range of relevant detail from both texts
4	• Synthesizes with clear understanding and provides an overview drawn from a range of relevant detail from both texts

Answers in the top mark band 'provide an overview'; this means they take a step back from the detail and consider the bigger picture of the texts. An overview works like the headline of an article or the summary on a weather forecast, giving the main points either before or after all the details have been considered. If there is a main difference to notice, commenting on it would show you can 'synthesize with clear understanding'.

Activity 4

The example student response opposite answers a question requiring the same skills as the question in Activity 3 but with a different focus:

> Explain what you learn about Llewelyn in both texts. **[4]**

1. Read the response carefully. With a partner, find examples of where it fulfils the top mark band criteria.

2. Look back over your own answer from Activity 3 explaining what you learn about the dog. Then use the Llewelyn example as a model either to write your own overview or to improve on the overview you have already written.

3. Swap your work with a partner and compare your overviews.

In the web text, Llewelyn is titled 'Prince'. In the Borrow extract, 'followers' suggests his leadership but not his royalty. The activity of Llewelyn is specific in the web text as he is out 'hunting'. The Borrow text describes his 'expedition'. In both texts, the important detail is that he leaves his baby. The Borrow text specifically says the baby is left 'under the care of his hound Gelert', which shows Llewelyn trusts that his dog will keep his son safe and makes his later action more shocking. In both texts, Llewelyn returns and sees the blood around the baby's tent (Borrow) and cot (web) and on his own dog, who is 'smeared' (web) and 'covered' (Borrow) with 'blood'. He wrongly interprets this as showing that his own dog has slaughtered his son and, in both extracts, due to his strong emotion, makes the rash decision of killing Gelert before he has the full facts. In Borrow, Llewelyn suffers a 'paroxysm of natural indignation'. The word 'natural' shows sympathy with his feelings of anger at this wicked deed. In the web text, 'frantic' suggests that Llewelyn hasn't thought his actions through. Llewelyn's hasty decision to kill Gelert before he has discovered him actually to be his son's protector and saviour is found in both texts. This is perhaps the most important part of the story, because it leads to the strong emotion Llewelyn feels when he realizes his error of judgement. In Borrow, he is said to feel 'conflicting emotions' of 'joy' that his son is actually alive and 'grief' at his responsibility for his dog's unnecessary death. The web text shows Llewelyn's reflection and 'remorse' at needlessly slaughtering his own dog and considers a part of the legend that Llewelyn 'is said never to have smiled again'.

5 Combining information: putting skills into practice

This unit will bring together your skills in combining evidence from different texts. The first extract is taken from an article by Mick Gradwell, former head of Lancashire Police CID, published in 2014 in the *Lancashire Evening Post*. The second extract was written by Elizabeth Keckley and is taken from her book *Behind the Scenes, or Thirty Years a Slave and Four Years in the White House*, first published in 1868.

Assessment Objective

- **AO1**
  - 2 Select and synthesize evidence from different texts.

Activity 1

Read the texts carefully and answer the following question:

> According to both texts, what are the ways in which people are treated as slaves/in slavery? **[4]**

Look back over the advice on page 78 about selecting a range of evidence and providing an overview before you start.

Extract 1

Anybody who thinks acts of slavery are now confined to the pages of history books would be very wrong.

Slavery is a modern day problem that doesn't just take place in far off places; it's a growing issue in this country. [...] Modern Slavery is what I would describe as a hidden crime because it can easily be overlooked and is often only discovered as a byproduct of another, entirely unrelated criminal investigation.

There have been recent cases discovered within sections of the travelling community, where alcoholic down and out men have allegedly been picked up off the street, forced to live in sheds and do unpaid labour for many years. [...] Perhaps unsurprisingly, the main victims are immigrants who have been trafficked to the UK.

There are quite horrific stories being uncovered about young women being conned into travelling to this country by being promised exciting work opportunities.

When they initially arrive, they are provided with free food and accommodation, while they apply for jobs that either don't exist or they are not qualified for.

After several weeks or months, those who have been providing them with free board then request

payment for their assistance. As they have no means to pay, pressure is placed on them to do work in lieu of payment and this leads to their sexual exploitation. [...]

Acts of slavery will be taking place in this area and it is important people consider reporting any suspicious activity they see.

Extract 2

Extract from *Behind the Scenes, or Thirty Years a Slave and Four Years in the White House* by Elizabeth Keckley

When I was about seven years old I witnessed, for the first time, the sale of a human being. We were living at Prince Edward, in Virginia, and master had just purchased his hogs for the winter, for which
5   he was unable to pay in full. To escape from his embarrassment it was necessary to sell one of the slaves. Little Joe, the son of the cook, was selected as the victim. His mother was ordered to dress him up in his Sunday clothes, and send him to the house. He
10 came in with a bright face, was placed in the scales, and was sold, like the hogs, at so much per pound. His mother was kept in ignorance of the transaction, but her suspicions were aroused.

When her son started for Petersburgh in the wagon,
15 the truth began to dawn upon her mind, and she pleaded piteously that her boy should not be taken from her; but master quieted her by telling her that he was simply going to town with the wagon, and would be back in the morning. Morning came, but little Joe
20 did not return to his mother. Morning after morning passed, and the mother went down to the grave without ever seeing her child again...

Activity 2

Swap your work with a partner to compare your answers.

1. Highlight relevant details they have drawn out from the texts.
2. Highlight the links made between the texts.
3. Look at the mark scheme provided on page 78. What mark would you give the answer? Give a target for improvement.

When you get your own work back, look carefully at the comments made. Then re-draft and improve your answer.

Activity 3

Make a list of three to five top tips you would give to someone who is struggling with combining evidence from two texts.

Tip Sometimes it is not the words which are hard to understand but how they have been used. You might not have heard the expression 'went down to the grave', but you can understand it by thinking 'around' the meanings of the words. You know that a grave is where someone is buried, so with thought you can get to the correct meaning of the expression, which is 'died'.

6 Writer's craft: language and tone

Assessment Objective

- **AO2**
  – 1a Comment on, explain and analyse how writers use language, using relevant subject terminology to support your views.

There are many possible ways you might be asked to explain, comment on and analyse how a writer has crafted their work in the Component 2 Reading exam. For example, questions such as: 'What impressions do you get of...?', 'What do you think and feel about...?', 'Explain how...', 'What are the writer's thoughts and feelings about...?', 'How does the writer...?'

These questions will often have bullet points which you need to follow too. An example might be, 'comment on the language or tone of the writer'. In this unit you are going to study a question which asks you to analyse the language a writer has used in two extracts. Remember: in an exam this would just be one part of a wider question on the techniques a writer can use; you might also be required to consider structure and other elements of the writer's craft.

Tip Always remember that questions on the writer's craft are a purposeful activity: they are asking you *how* a writer achieves a certain effect or influences you to do or think something. It doesn't mean a list of features with no explanation. You must show an understanding of the words and examples you select. Also, although you will be rewarded for using appropriate vocabulary, simply labelling similes or short sentences, for example, when they are not relevant to the question being asked is meaningless. Remember: AO2 asks for 'relevant subject terminology'.

Activity 1

Promotional materials like leaflets and websites often use persuasive language about a place or experience in order to sell it to their target audience.

Read the two extracts from the 'Predator Experience' leaflet.

1. Make a list of words and phrases which help to persuade the reader that the experience will be exciting and memorable.

2. Compare your list with a partner or another pair and add relevant words and phrases to your own list.

Extract 1

EAGLE EXPERIENCE

Experience the freedom of Lakeland, as we transport you to the fells to fly both species of British eagles. Following a short walk, experience our iconic Golden Eagle as he soars in the mountains then swoops to land gently on to your gloved hand. Our White-tailed Sea Eagle, the largest British raptor, will fly dramatically for you, again, gently landing on to your glove. After lunch (provided), you will fly the largest of the owl family, the European Eagle Owl and the Verreaux Eagle Owl.
Full Day. Minimum age 16 yrs.

Extract 2

EXPERIENCE DAY

Experience Days are a fantastic way for you to meet many different types of falcons, hawks and owls. We will introduce you to precision predators and some real characters! Where possible you will fly the birds yourself including our Eagle Owl 'Crumble' and our Harris Hawk 'Jarreth'. We will teach you the falconers knot and how to pick up and handle birds of prey. Experience Days are fun and informative. Available in full or half days. Minimum age 12 years.

EXPERIENCE DAY

Experience Days are a fantastic way for you to meet many different types of falcons, hawks and owls. We will introduce you to precision predators and some real characters! Where possible you will fly the birds yourself including our Eagle Owl 'Crumble' and our Harris Hawk 'Jarreth'. We will teach you the falconers knot and how to pick up and handle birds of prey. Experience Days are fun and informative. Available in full or half days. Minimum age 12 yrs.

HAWK WALK

Walking through the stunning Lakeland countryside you will be given the opportunity to fly our team of hawks and interact with the pack. Our hawks follow us flying tree to glove as we stroll along. Hawk Walks are a great way to be close to raptors and observe their opportunistic natural behaviours. Duration 1 hour. Suitable for all ages.

Activity 2

Remember that in an exam you might be asked a question such as:

> How does the writer make the experiences sound exciting and memorable? **[10]**

To help you to decide which words and phrases are relevant, keep the question in mind. Ask yourself 'Does this word persuade me that the experience is exciting or memorable?' If it doesn't, it's not relevant. If it does, ask 'Why?' to help you comment on the reasons it persuades you.

Look back over your list of selected words and phrases from Activity 1:

1. Make sure they are all relevant.

2. Note down a few words to explain why they persuade you.

Activity 3

Now you are going to write your answer to the question in Activity 2.

1. Look at these relevant techniques and quotations from the extracts. Can you add any of your own?

   - Adjectives carefully chosen to describe a noun as impressive: 'iconic Golden Eagle', 'precision predators'

   - Superlatives designed to impress and persuade you that this can't be bettered: 'largest British raptor', 'largest of the owl family'

   - Links or patterns: the contrast of the adverbs describing how the Sea Eagle flies 'dramatically' but lands 'gently'

   - Groups of words giving the same effect: the present tense verbs 'soars' and 'swoops' used to visualize the flight of the Golden Eagle

   - Second-person pronoun to put the reader in control of the birds: 'for you', 'your gloved hand', 'you will fly'

   - Suggestions that creatures have real personality: 'some real characters!'

   - Expressions which put the reader closer to the animals: 'on your gloved hand', 'on to your glove'; and verbs which emphasize the closeness with the birds: 'pick up' and 'handle'

   - Adjectives which suggest energy/enthusiasm or what a great time it will be: 'fantastic', 'fun'

2. Comment on three language features, either from the list above or your own ideas. Explain how they help to persuade the reader that the experience will be exciting and memorable.

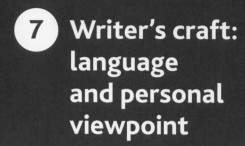

7 Writer's craft: language and personal viewpoint

Assessment Objective

- **AO2**
  - 1a Comment on, explain and analyse how writers use language, using relevant subject terminology to support your views.

A personal viewpoint is often given by the writer in the source texts in Component 2. Their language choices shape their tone. They might use humour or be serious and direct. Likewise, they choose their words carefully to shape the reader's perspective on a topic. Understanding the tone of the writing can give you a better sense of what the writer really thinks or feels about a topic, helping you to write a sharper answer to a question about the writer's craft.

Activity 1

The extract below was taken from an online *Telegraph* newspaper article. Tom Cox, the writer, has just met a lady who has complimented him on his dog. He is explaining that the dog is not his but from a website called BorrowMyDoggy.

Read the extract through carefully.

1. Explain how Cox feels admitting he met his dog 'online'. Give evidence for your view.

2. Track through the article and list the benefits the BorrowMyDoggy website can bring to dog lovers who can't own a dog and the benefits to dogs.

 HOME BLOG CONTACT

I take a slight breath, although perhaps not as deep as the one I might have taken before saying the same thing a month or two earlier. 'We met… online.'

It has taken a while for me to be comfortable in admitting I met my part-time dog on the internet, but I'm OK with it now, and so is Billy. Of course, others may have a problem with it, but in the end it's their problem, not ours. Way back in the previous decade I borrowed dogs from people I met in real life. […] Since then, the lives of humans and dogs have become more virtual, and different ways to meet dogs have become more acceptable. In spring, I had moved to a new part of the country – Devon – and my initial attempts to meet dogs to borrow had proved unsuccessful. 'Have you tried BorrowMyDoggy?' a friend suggested.

BorrowMyDoggy is the first site of its kind, and aims to provide an inexpensive, mutually beneficial arrangement for owners who need minders for their dogs, and dogless folk, such as me, who love dogs but prefer to love them in a part-time sort of way. It was founded two years ago as a weekend project by Les Cochrane, an RSPCA volunteer, and Rikke Rosenlund, a dog lover who could never have a dog as a child because of her mother's allergy. Rosenlund hit on the idea while she was looking after a neighbour's labrador; it is her belief that 'there is no need for a dog to be home alone, or for people to pay for a dog walker on a lovely Sunday or to pay for kennels when there are lots of people who adore dogs but can't have them due to work, or travel, or other reasons.'

Activity 2

A question you might face about this extract is:

> How does Cox portray the website BorrowMyDoggy as a great thing for people who love dogs but don't want to own one of their own? **[10]**

Listing the benefits in Activity 1 means you have already chosen the relevant details. To answer this question you must also comment on the language which makes the service sound great.

1. Read the student responses below. Decide which response selects and quotes precise examples of language.

2. Give a reason why precise quotation is important.

Student 1

The writer says that it is better now that people are OK with people borrowing dogs. He says, 'different ways to meet dogs have become more acceptable'.

Student 2

Cox argues it is easier to borrow a dog in a 'virtual' way now it's become more 'acceptable'. This presents the website as a great thing for the 'dogless' as it agrees that some people love dogs and want an easy way of enjoying their company if they don't have a dog-owning friend.

Activity 3

Link each benefit you listed in Activity 1 to key words or a language feature which shows the BorrowMyDoggy website as a 'great thing'. Then use Student 2's response above as a model to write your answer. You might consider:

* words about money
* negative words like 'no', 'never'
* words describing dog lovers
* lists of reasons some people can't own a dog
* words creating a positive image of walking a dog.

(8) Writer's craft: language and expert opinion

Assessment Objective

- **AO2**

  – 1a Comment on, explain and analyse how writers use language, using relevant subject terminology to support your views.

Sometimes a text in the Component 2 exam might give the views of an expert in their field. The writer of the text might themselves be the expert because they have experienced what they are writing about first hand, or they might quote people who have done research or have experience.

The expert might use subject-specific vocabulary or facts which show their own knowledge of the topic. This unit will help you to analyse how expert views can be given in an article, which is something you may be asked to do as part of a wider exam question on the writer's craft.

Activity 1

The extract below is taken from an article by Juliette Garside published in the *Guardian* online newspaper. You will use it to answer the following question:

> How does Juliette Garside argue that children are trendsetters in 'shaping communications'? Comment on what she says and how she says it. **[10]**

Track through the article carefully and list the reasons Garside gives to argue that children are trendsetters for shaping communications.

HOME   NEWS   ARTICLES   DOWNLOADS

Ofcom: six-year-olds understand digital technology better than adults

Juliette Garside

They may not know who Steve Jobs was or even how to tie their own shoelaces, but the average six-year-old child understands more about digital technology than a 45-year-old adult, according to an authoritative new report published on Thursday.

The advent of broadband in the year 2000 has created a generation of digital natives, the communication watchdog Ofcom* says in its annual study of British consumers. Born in the new millennium, these children have never known the dark ages of dial up internet, and the youngest are learning how to operate smartphones or tablets before they are able to talk.

'These younger people are shaping communications,' said Jane Rumble, Ofcom's media research head. 'As a result of growing up in the digital age, they are developing fundamentally different communication habits from older generations. [...]'

The most remarkable change is in time spent talking by phone. Two decades ago, teenagers devoted their evenings to monopolising the home telephone line, dissecting love affairs and friendships in conversations that lasted for hours.

For those aged 12 to 15, phone calls account for just 3% of time spent communicating through any device. For all adults, this rises to 20%, and for young adults it is still three times as high at 9%. Today's children do the majority of their remote socialising by sending written messages or through shared photographs and videos.

*Ofcom – an organization which regulates communications providers such as BT or Sky

Activity 2

There are a number of language choices in this article which show its expert focus and which help Garside's argument. Look at the following table of methods and quote an example for each one from the article:

Method	Example
Specific technological vocabulary: 'digital natives'	
An expert on the subject: 'Ofcom'	
Words which focus on the value of the expert's findings: 'authoritative'	
Facts	
Direct quotations from the authors of the study	
Use of the verb 'are' to show a sense of certainty	
Adjectives which point out the change as worthy of notice: 'remarkable'	

Activity 3

Choose three methods from the table in Activity 2 and explain how Garside uses them to support her argument that children are the trendsetters in 'shaping communications'. For example:

> Garside says that children 'born in the new millennium' are 'digital natives'. This helps to begin her argument that children are the trendsetters because it shows how comfortable they are with the technology. It is not necessary for them to learn to use mobiles and tablets; they have grown up around them and so can use them more effectively than the older generation, even 'before they can talk'.

Remember to:

- use quotations precisely
- say specifically what the effect or impact on the reader is
- use the correct label for the method used (if there is one)
- link your answer to the words in the question.

9 Writer's craft: structure

Assessment Objective

- **AO2**
  – 1b Comment on, explain and analyse how writers use structure, using relevant subject terminology to support your views.

The English word *structure* comes from the Latin word *structura* meaning 'thing built'. It might seem a bit odd to say that a writer is like a builder, but when you think about structure in terms of writing, the thing built is the article, leaflet or blog. The writer has made choices about how it goes together so it is strong, just like a construction worker must make their building strong. Of course, the writer doesn't build with bricks or metal but organizes their writing with headings, sub-headings, paragraphs, topic sentences, sections, bullet points, spider diagrams, tables and lists.

In an exam you might comment on structure under a wider question about the writer's craft. The activities here will help you to consider how you would analyse structure as part of a question such as:

> How has the writer made the leaflet persuasive and informative? **[10]**

Kendal once again bursts into life with (mostly free!) street performances from across the world.

On Saturday you can enjoy the delights of Mintfest on the Streets. Always one of the highlights of the festival, the whole town ripples with laughter as a tidal-wave of artists and performers roll onto the streets to offer daytime delights.

Sunday's programme is located predominantly around Abbot Hall Park. Bring a picnic or buy some treats from the catering stalls and soak up the ambience of park life whilst you enjoy a host of circus, dance, theatre and walkabout performances.

There are plenty of treats available in the evenings this year. European and UK companies offer enchantments, excitement and awe with some unique and beautiful shows, and after the sun (yes – it's coming this year!) goes down, join our festival club in the Brewery Malt Room for a few drinks, quirky cabaret and dancing until late.

If music is more your cup of tea, the Brewery gardens will once again be swinging to the rhythms of the world on Saturday evening and Sunday afternoon.

The provisional detailed programme is now online and tickets (where needed) will be on sale in early July.

Highlights include:

- Acrobatic aerial excitement from FullStop Acrobatics (UK/NL)
- The extraordinary creatures of La Menagerie by La Compagnie DeFo (BEL)
- New commissions from UK companies including Marc Brew and Wet Picnic through the Without Walls programme
- Contemporary circus cabaret from Les Krilati (FRA)
- See Kendal in a new light with an extraordinary site-specific wandering performance of Dead Ends by Ishmael Falke & Sandrina Lindgren (ISR/FIN)
- A poetic musical installation in the ruins of Kendal Castle by Tuig (NL).

We hope you'll join us!

www.lakesalive.org

Activity 1

Read the extract from the Mintfest leaflet.

1. List techniques used to build or structure the text.

2. Check your list against that of a partner or another pair. Add any extra techniques to your own list.

Key terms

Topic sentence: the key sentence that explains what a paragraph is about
Call to action: an instruction often found at the end of an advert, leaflet or charity letter such as 'Don't delay!'

Activity 2

Now you are going to practise commenting on the structural techniques used in this text by answering this question:

> How does the writer structure the leaflet to make it persuasive and informative? **[10]**

You must explain how each structural technique helps the information given in the leaflet to be informative or persuasive, or both.

1. Working with a partner, decide on whether the bullet points used help the leaflet to be informative, persuasive or both. Give a reason for your decision.

2. Write up your ideas in a paragraph which answers the exam question. Remember to use precise quotation and comment on how the technique helps to inform or persuade the reader.

3. Compare your answer with the student comments below.

> The bullet points help the informative purpose of the leaflet as they clearly display a list of the highlights. Showing a number of points also gives a choice to the reader which persuades you that there will be lots of exciting events to captivate different interests of the audience.

4. Give yourself a target about how to comment on structure such as: label a specific feature, draw a link to the purpose of the text, or comment on the effect on the audience.

5. Keeping your target in mind, write a paragraph analysing how three of the following techniques are used in the leaflet to make it persuasive and informative:

- Opening summary sentence
- Time indicators/**topic sentences** to start each paragraph
- Sub-heading
- **Call to action**
- Website

10 Writer's craft: achieving effects

Assessment Objective

● **AO2**

– 1c Comment on, explain and analyse how writers achieve effects, using relevant subject terminology to support your views.

> **Tip** If you are already familiar with a topic or character from an exam text, make sure you only talk about them as presented in the text. Don't bring in additional information or opinion.

Writers make careful language choices to create a certain picture of a place or character. In the exam you can be asked to give your impressions of a character, or comment on how an issue, place or character is presented. There are two parts to success in this area: 1) staying focused on the text to help you select explicit details and implicit meanings relevant to the question; and 2) commenting on the effect the writer is giving through the words and phrases used.

Remember that in the exam you may need to comment on how several elements of the writer's craft have been used together to achieve certain effects. In this unit you will concentrate on how language can be used to achieve effects.

You will explore how the writer of the following extract presents the Stig, the racing driver character from the TV programme *Top Gear*.

Activity 1

Annotations are great for selecting words and phrases and making notes on an exam text. The annotations on the first paragraph opposite respond to this question:

> Explain what impressions you get of the Stig in this article. Comment on what is said about him, the words and phrases used. **[10]**

Read the first paragraph and the annotations.

1. With a partner, discuss what makes these words and phrases relevant details for the question.

2. Discuss the ideas/notes with a partner to check your understanding.

3. Write up the annotations in a paragraph to answer the question.

You might want to comment on specific words selected or a mood that is created by a certain line.

> **Tip** Not everything a writer does has a label, such as 'simile' or 'structure'. You might want to comment on specific words a writer has chosen or a mood that is created by a certain line. If they have created an effect in the text which is relevant to the question you are answering, this is a valid comment.

Register   Log in

Search

Home | Business | World | UK | Sports

The Stig and I: My Top Gear adventure

Tim Dowling

I am standing in the car park outside the Top Gear studio hangar in Dunsfold Park in Surrey, trying to poke my hand far enough up the inside of my crash helmet to straighten my ears. A white Porsche GT3 idles throatily beside me, passenger door open. Behind the wheel is the Stig, visor down, looking impassive and a little menacing. I swallow hard, climb in and shut the door.

'How's it going?' I say. The Stig stares straight ahead, and says nothing.

I know the Stig isn't supposed to talk – that, strictly speaking, he's a role without lines – but in person his silence is still unnerving. Even when you have your picture taken with him, the Stig only responds to the photographer's instructions when they're delivered through an intermediary.

We drive a short distance to the edge of the Top Gear track, about 50 metres past the starting line. The sun beats down on the tarmac, sending up shimmering waves of heat so thick they cast shadows.

'Nice day for it,' I say. The Stig stares straight ahead, and says nothing. We can't pull out yet, because there's another car on the track – we have to wait our turn. After a few moments, the unnerving silence becomes merely awkward. Imagine waiting at a bus stop with the Ghost of Christmas Yet to Come.

'looking Impassive': not bothered. Showing no emotion. Hard to read

'I swallow hard': Physical response of writer to Stig suggests fear/nerves: Stig is a character to be feared, fits with 'menacing'

'a little menacing': something scary about him, associated with evil or being teased. Makes writer (and reader) feel uneasy, nervous of him

Activity 2

The comments below are written by a student about the last line from the article on page 91. They would score highly for accuracy using the mark scheme and begin to analyse how the writer creates the mysterious impression of the Stig.

> The final line continues the impression of the Stig as a mysterious character by comparing the Stig with 'the Ghost of Christmas Yet to Come'. Even if the reader doesn't know anything about this specific ghost they will understand that the reference to a supernatural creature brings a spooky feel to the Stig.

1. Write down the words used to analyse the language and structure in the student paragraph above: 'by comparing... with...', 'the reference to... brings...'.

2. How many of these words and phrases did you use in your paragraph for Activity 1? What others have you used? Write them down and share ideas with a partner so you can use them in your own writing.

3. Compare the quality of your comments with the student response above. Looking at the mark scheme below, would your comments score more highly? Would your mark be lower? What are your reasons?

4. Give yourself a target for improvement.

Mark	Criteria
0	• Nothing worthy of credit
1–2	• Identifies and begins to comment on some examples • May struggle to engage with the text and/or the question
3–4	• Identifies and gives straightforward comments on some examples • Simply identifies some subject terminology
5–6	• Explains how a number of different examples create impressions • Begins to show some understanding of how language and structure are used to achieve effects • Begins to use relevant subject terminology accurately to support their comments
7–8	• Makes accurate comments about how a range of different examples create impressions • Begins to analyse how language and structure are used to achieve effects • Subject terminology is used accurately to support comments effectively
9–10	• Makes accurate and perceptive comments about how a wide range of different examples create impressions • Provides detailed analysis of how language and structure are used to achieve effects • Subtleties of the writer's technique are explored • Well-considered, accurate use of subject terminology supports comments effectively

Activity 3

Now make notes on the middle section of the article. Then write up a full answer to the question on page 90.

- Remember to select material relevant to the question: the impressions of Stig.
- Use the phrases you wrote down to explore your ideas.
- Act on your target from Activity 2.
- Group together quotations which give the same impression.

Activity 4

Now you are going to put your understanding of how to select ideas for discussion to the test. The newspaper article on the right, printed in the 1800s, describes how William Dale was transported to Botany Bay in Australia, aged 14, for robbery. Read the extract through carefully.

1. Work with a partner to explain the meaning of the following words from the context of the sentence: proprictyas, backsliders, remonstrated, infamy.

2. Check your definitions with another group and/or a dictionary.

3. Track through the text carefully. Make notes on changes you notice in William Dale's character. Support each comment with textual reference.

William Dale was reared within 10 miles of London. When he was 14 years of age, he was apprenticed to a Tinsmith, near Fleet-Market, and for the first four years of his apprenticeship he conducted himself with such proprietyas to become a great favourite with his Master. Such was William's early prospects;- now, mark what follows, and behold the reward of such as do wickedly and the sure and certain punishment that awaits those who are backsliders from the paths of religion and honesty. It was his sad misfortune to form an acquaintance with a set of young, loose, idle fellows, who take delight in nothing but frequenting public-houses, and have no pleasure in their business, but consider it as a grievous burden upon them. It was not long before William began to neglect his work and stop out all night frequently. His parents remonstrated with him, but in vain, he was deaf to their remonstrance, and so went on in his guilty career, till to crown his infamy, he turned a regular thief, and was with three others, apprehended robbing a Merchant's house in the city. [...] He and his miserable companions were convicted to Botany-Bay.

Activity 5

Use your notes from Activity 4 to answer this question:

> Explain how William Dale's change in character is presented. Comment on what is said and the words used. **[10]**

- Remember that similar techniques are used to create effects in 19th-century texts as in 21st-century texts, such as descriptive adjectives, verbs and adverbs or metaphor.
- Look back at the strategies advised in Activity 3 above.

Tip If you are asked to comment on the change in a character, remember to be explicit about what they are like at the beginning of the extract and at the end. Avoid vague statements like 'The change in Dale is shown by…'. Instead you need to say what they change from and to.

11 Writer's craft: influencing the reader

Assessment Objective

- **AO2**

  – 1d Comment on, explain and analyse how writers influence readers, using relevant subject terminology to support your views.

Influence is sometimes considered a feature of powerful people who make you do or think something you didn't necessarily want to. Writers and their writing are also powerful when they influence or change the minds of their reader by making you see from their point of view. This can be tested in the exam with questions like: 'How does the writer persuade or convince you that…?' or 'What are the writer's thoughts and feelings about…?' In this unit you will analyse how a writer makes a case using word choices which give their impression of a topic.

Activity 1

Read through the headline and first paragraph of the article below. Write a short paragraph to explain how they summarize the writer Alex Needham's view about music.

Artist creates space for public to hear music

Alex Needham

Live concert venues and nightclubs still stud city centres, and music pours out of phone and computer speakers, but public spaces where one can simply sit and listen to a record have become rare to non-existent – until now.

On Friday in Berlin, the artist Wolfgang Tillmans will open a 'playback room' in his gallery, Between Bridges. It's designed to do two things – to allow listeners to hear a record on a top-of-the-range stereo, and to give pop music the same love and reverence that galleries give to visual art.

'Some records are just perfect artworks, but you just cannot go anywhere to listen to the way the musicians heard it at the mastering stage,' said Tillmans, who won the Turner prize in 2000. 'While you can play them on your stereo or iPhone there is never a space dedicated to them and you can never listen in studio quality.' […]

Tillmans said the experience of hearing the music on a top-end stereo 'tickles nerves that are not usually touched… it's mind-blowing when you hear things you've never heard before in a record.' […]

Tillmans said he hoped that other arts institutions would follow suit and open their own listening rooms; that galleries would open themselves up to music in the way they embraced his photographs.

Activity 2

Now read the rest of the article and select key ideas relevant to the following question:

> Tillmans argues that pop music should have 'public spaces' where people 'can simply sit and listen to a record'. How does the article convince you of this view? Comment on what is said and the way Tillmans gets his argument across. **[10]**

Make it clear in your writing whether you are quoting from the writer, Alex Needham, or the artist, Wolfgang Tillmans.

Activity 3

One of the key ways Needham influences his reader is by arguing that music has a right to be heard on a 'top-of-the-range stereo' and like a 'perfect artwork' needs to be displayed in a gallery. Track through the text and list the words Needham and Tillmans use which suggest a love of music.

Activity 4

The student response below explains how one of the key words from the article suggests the writer's enthusiasm for music.

1. Work with a partner and list three things this answer does to explain how the word 'reverence' influences the reader.

2. Use this response as a model to write up three of the words you listed in Activity 3.

Perhaps one of the most significant words to speak of the enthusiasm both Needham and Tillmans show for music is the word 'reverence'. Needham relies on its meaning of 'respecting something as if a god' to show how important music is for him. This also justifies the need for somewhere that the music can 'tickle nerves that are not usually touched' such as is offered by Tillmans' playback room. This physical reaction to hearing the music draws a parallel with the feelings of being 'touched' that a religious person might have in a place of worship. It influences the reader to see the value of music being played publicly by suggesting it can have the same profound effect as a god or religion.

95

Activity 5

Now read the extract below from Simon Kelner's newspaper article 'Commuters of Britain: unite against this aural tyranny'.

1. Using your own words, summarize his argument by completing the sentence 'Kelner argues that…'.

2. Make a list of the reasons he gives to support his argument.

HOME   BUSINESS   TECHNOLOGY   SCIENCE   LIFESTYLE   SPORTS   ENTERTAINMENT

Commuters of Britain: unite against this aural tyranny!

Simon Kelner

Instead of a quiet carriage, why don't we have a noisy carriage?

Very occasionally in this space, I manage to capture the mood of a nation. This happened last week when I lamented the end of quiet carriages on trains, and generally fulminated[1] about people using their mobile phones in public. Why should we be forced to listen to others' dreary conversations, I asked? The reaction this prompted, overwhelmingly positive, led me to believe I am on to something. This is a subject a lot of people care about. There was a time not that long ago when you could smoke a cigarette on a train, and now it would be regarded as an offence against humanity. Could the same happen to making mobile phone calls in public spaces? […]

One of my respondents on Twitter suggested I start a campaign against mobile calls on public transport. But it's hard to know where to start. You can't really legislate[2] against breaches of politeness. Nevertheless, politeness should be the norm. Instead of a quiet carriage, why don't we have a noisy carriage? Quietness is standard, but if you want to make a call on your mobile, there's a special carriage available. […] Smokers used to be banished to their own filthy carriage: let's do the same with slaves of the mobile.

[1] fulminated – protested loudly and angrily
[2] legislate – to make or pass laws

Activity 6

An exam question which might be asked on this extract is:

> How does Kelner try to convince the reader that we should ban mobile phone use on public transport? Comment on what he says and the ways he puts his ideas across. **[10]**

In Activity 5 you listed reasons Kelner gives to support his view. Now focus on 'the ways he puts his ideas across'.

1. List the key words and phrases Kelner uses to persuade you of his view. Specify what language technique is being used if there is one, for example, exaggeration.

2. Group the methods under these effects and add other examples:

   a) Showing a united hate for public mobile phone use, for example, 'the mood of a nation'

   b) Drawing a comparison with smoking on trains, for example, 'an offence against humanity'

   c) Seeking agreement from the reader, for example, use of a rhetorical question and ideas about politeness.

Activity 7

You are going to write up your answer.

1. First, read the mark scheme below carefully. What mark would you usually aim for? Write two challenging but achievable targets to try to improve your mark.

2. Use your notes to write up your answer, focusing carefully on your targets.

3. Mark your work using the mark scheme and assess whether you met your targets.

Tip Group language features which have a similar effect, rather than writing about them individually, to show that you understand how the devices work together to influence the reader in a certain way.

Mark	Criteria
0	• Nothing worthy of credit
1–2	• Identifies and begins to comment on some examples of the writer's argument • May struggle to engage with the text and/or the question
3–4	• Identifies and gives straightforward comments on some examples of the writer's argument • Simply identifies some subject vocabulary
5–6	• Explains how a number of different examples from the writer's argument persuade • Begins to show some understanding of how language and structure are used to influence the reader • Begins to use relevant subject vocabulary accurately to support their comments
7–8	• Makes accurate comments about how a range of different examples from the writer's argument persuade • Begins to analyse how language and structure are used to influence the reader • Subject terminology is used accurately to support comments effectively
9–10	• Makes accurate and perceptive comments about how a wide range of different examples from the writer's argument persuade • Provides detailed analysis of how language and structure are used to influence the reader • Subtleties of the writer's technique are explored • Well-considered, accurate use of subject vocabulary supports comments effectively

12 Writer's craft: combining elements

Assessment Objective

- **AO2**
  – Explain, comment on and analyse how writers use language and structure to achieve effects and influence readers, using relevant subject terminology to support your views.

The activities here are going to help you analyse all of the elements of writer's craft which are tested in the Component 2 exam. The letter by Charles Dickens below is written to call for hangings to be private affairs. His description of the crowd who gather for this kind of entertainment is used as one way of arguing that there is something quite inhuman about this kind of public spectacle.

Activity 1

1. Scan through the text and decide whether we are meant to like the crowd that Dickens describes. Consult the glossary at the bottom to check the meaning of unfamiliar words as you read through.

2. What impressions do you get of the crowd? Support each impression with evidence.

I believe that a sight so inconceivably awful as the wickedness and levity¹ of the immense crowd collected at that execution could be imagined by no man, and could be presented in no heathen land under the sun. The horrors of the gibbet² and of the crime which brought the wretched murderers to it, faded in my mind before the atrocious bearing, looks and language, of the assembled spectators.   5

When I came upon the scene at midnight, the shrillness of the cries and howls that were raised from time to time, denoting that they came from a concourse of boys and girls already assembled in the best places, made my blood run cold. [...]   10

When the day dawned, thieves, low prostitutes, ruffians³ and vagabonds⁴ of every kind, flocked on to the ground, with every variety of offensive and foul behaviour. [...]Fightings, faintings, whistlings, [...] brutal jokes, tumultuous⁵ demonstrations of   15 indecent delight when swooning women were dragged out of the crowd by the police with their dresses disordered, gave a new zest to the general entertainment. When the sun rose brightly—as it did—it gilded thousands upon thousands of upturned faces, so inexpressibly odious⁶ in their brutal mirth⁷   20 or callousness⁸, that a man had cause to feel ashamed of the shape he wore, and to shrink from himself, as fashioned in the image of the Devil. When the two miserable creatures who attracted all this ghastly sight about them were turned quivering into the air, there was no more emotion, no more   25 pity, no more thought that two immortal souls had gone to judgement, no more restraint in any of the previous obscenities⁹, than if the name of Christ had never been heard in this world, and there were no belief among men but that they perished like the beasts.   30

¹levity – a humorous attitude towards serious matters

²gibbet – the gallows structure where bodies or dying criminals were hung for public display

³ruffians – violent or lawless people

⁴vagabonds – people without a settled home or regular work

⁵tumultuous – making a loud or confused noise

⁶odious – extremely unpleasant

⁷mirth – merriment or laughter

⁸callousness – unfeeling or cruel behaviour

⁹obscenities – indecent or offensive actions or expressions

Activity

The following question allows you to comment on all of the elements of writer's craft – language, structure, effects and influence:

> How does Dickens create an impression of the crowd as awful and wicked? Comment on what he says about the crowd and the words and phrases he uses about them. **[10]**

This text is challenging but tracking through each sentence reveals lots of details to help you answer this question. The table below identifies and explains some of the techniques used in the first three sentences.

1. Discuss and check your understanding of the techniques listed in the table from the first three sentences of the text.

2. Copy and complete the table by selecting the techniques and details used by Dickens in sentences 4–7 (lines 12–30).

Line number	Techniques or details used by Dickens to create an impression of the crowd as awful and wicked
1–4	He uses references to the lack of religion in a structural way: he frames the extract by placing these references in the first and last lines.
4–7	Dickens emphasizes how awful the spectators are by saying that they are so bad they make him forget the gallows where the people are to be hung.
8–11	He portrays the young people out at midnight like wolves or vampires at bewitching hour. He uses a superlative to show the type of seats they have. The physical effect on Dickens is chilling.
12–14	
14–18	
18–23	
23–30	

Activity 3

Now use the techniques listed in the table in Activity 2 to write up your answer to the question. You might choose to comment on the first three sentences using the techniques listed in the table or choose three you have found yourself to give you more of a challenge.

- First find textual evidence to support each technique.
- Then develop your analysis in detail.
- Make sure you comment on how the language and structure have been used to create effects and to influence the reader's thoughts about the crowd.
- Use the mark scheme on page 97 to mark your work and give yourself a target for improvement.

Activity 4

Now you are going to plan and find all of the details you need to write an answer to another exam question. Follow the tips in the flow diagram below to answer this question on the extract opposite:

> Ellen E Jones describes a number of emotions in her review of BBC1's *DIY SOS The Big Build*. How does she make the reader share in these emotions?
>
> You should comment on what she says and the words/phrases she uses. **[10]**

1. **First make a plan:**
   a. Read the question carefully and decide what you need to look for or list on your first read through the text.
   b. Select the ideas and supporting details you need from the text.
   c. Decide how to organize or group your ideas.

2. **Then begin to write:**
   a. Make sure you make specific comments about the particular emotions Jones feels.
   b. Use short precise quotations to show the examiner you can focus on the exact words which have an influence.
   c. Explain the meaning, effect and/or influence of key words.
   d. Comment on whether you think the text is effective in making you share any particular emotion(s).

3. **Carefully check that your work:**
   a. makes sense – that no ideas/quotations are left unexplained
   b. shows a clear understanding of Jones's emotions
   c. shows a clear understanding of the words and phrases used
   d. comments on how the text affects or influences the reader.

TV | Soaps | Reality TV | Documentaries | Music | Movies

Home / TV / Reviews

DIY: SOS: the Big Build, BBC1

Ellen E Jones

A new series of DIY: SOS: the Big Build (BBC1) also provided a happy ending for John and June Finlay, a couple from Sunderland who had been living like prisoners in their own kitchen since June's mobility was reduced by serious illness four years ago.

Nick Knowles and the gang came to the rescue, transforming their two-bed house into a wheelchair-accessible haven.

All the volunteer wrangling and heartstring-tugging isn't native to the show's format – they've borrowed it from the US show Extreme Makeover: Home Edition – but Knowles is a natural at it, all the same. You could see the impact his motivational speech had on the workmen and he summed up John's tenacious* support for his wife of 35 years with these touching words: 'When you think about it, this is a love story. Not a fairytale love story, or a Hollywood love story, this is a down-in-the-trenches love story... John just would not give up on June.'

Most important item in your DIY: SOS watching tool box? A large box of tissues.

*tenacious – clinging firmly to rights or principles

13 Comparing views

Assessment Objective

- **AO3**
  – Compare writers' ideas and perspectives, as well as how these are conveyed, across two or more texts.

A question which will often come at the end of the exam asks you to compare two texts. You will have already read both texts in the exam so you'll be familiar with them. The ideas you need to select for this question might overlap slightly with other questions on the paper, but don't worry if you feel you might be repeating points you've already written. You do need to make sure you focus carefully on selecting only material which is relevant to this question. You will be specifically asked to *compare* the things the two writers have said on a topic, which means drawing out the similarities and differences in what they say and how they say it.

We will look at this and how it is different from questions which might ask you to *combine* or *synthesize* information on two texts.

This type of question will often tell you the focus for your comparison in the first line, saying something like 'Both of these texts are about…' or 'In both of these texts the writers give their views on…'. Therefore, you'll know only to comment on that given topic. Then there are two skills you'll need to show as you compare. You need to:

- pick out similar and different things the writers say about the topic
- write about the styles of the writing or how the writers put their views or information together.

Activity

So far you've learned that there are two types of question on the Component 2 paper which need you to write about two texts. You may like to look back over pages 76–79 which guide you through the skill of 'combining information from two texts' before you complete the task below.

The skills on the right are needed in the comparison question and/or the combining information question. Read through skills A–G carefully with a partner.

Draw up a table and write in the skills according to whether they are things you must do for the combining question, the comparison question or both. The first one is done as an example for you.

A	Read and comment on two different sources.
B	Select details relevant to the question.
C	Give a range of ideas.
D	Use quotations to support your comments.
E	Explore similarities and differences.
F	Comment on and compare the language used by the writers.
G	Use comparative vocabulary such as 'both', 'whereas', 'however'.

Combining	Comparison	Both
		A. Read and comment on two different sources.

You should now have a good sense of what is expected of you in this question, so it's time to put it into practice.

The following texts on page 104 are both about child labour and the issues around young children working. The extracts may be shorter than the texts you are likely to get in the exam but are a useful starting place to learn more about how to handle the comparison question. Extract 1 is taken from a web article called 'Gasp! The Benefits of Child Labour in the Developing World' by Lindsay Melnick. Extract 2 is from Lydia Child's book *The American Frugal Housewife* written in 1832.

You are now going to be guided step by step on a way to approach the question below.

> Both writers give their views on child labour. Compare the following:
>
> - the writers' attitudes to child labour
> - how they get across their arguments. **[10]**

Activity

1. Make a table in your book like the one below:

Extract 1	Extract 2

2. Read each extract carefully. Make a note of the intended reader and purpose of each text.

3. Track through Extract 1. List the things which the writer says about children working in column one of your table. Leave two lines in between each detail as you write the ideas down. Rule off your table under your final idea.

4. Then track through Extract 2. If you come across ideas in the second text which deal with a similar issue to those in Extract 1 (but don't necessarily agree), write them on the same row. If it's a different idea, write it in the rows below where you ruled off.

5. Highlight any key words which are similar in the table; for example, words which link to:

   a) helping the family/others   **c)** playing

   b) money   **d)** education/teaching.

6. Next make a decision about whether you think each text supports child labour or not. Check your ideas with a partner before you move on. If you have disagreements work out where they come from. Has one of you missed something, a subtlety in the argument, maybe? Or has one of you read or interpreted something wrongly? Ask your teacher if you are still unsure.

7. Write an opening sentence to your answer using comparative language which gives an overview of the views held in each text.

Tip **Audience:** To decide on who the text is aimed at you need to consider who the ideas in the text would interest. Are the ideas general, to appeal to a wider readership, or geared towards a specific gender or interest group?

Purpose: Remember that purpose means the job or the function of the text. Is it: Giving you information? Persuading you to do something? Advising how to do something? Trying to change your opinion? Something else?

Extract **1**

Gasp! The Benefits of Child Labour in the Developing World

Lindsay Melnick

If asked, most people in our society will tell you that they are dead set against the concept of child labour. They look disapprovingly at developing countries where young children perform manual labour for long hours when they should be in school learning. Yes, children should be in school. Yes, they should be out playing with friends and enjoying their childhood.

However, we do not live in a perfect world. Child labour is pervasive[1] for the simple reason that impoverished[2] households who cannot meet their basic needs may depend on the income of their children for survival. In many cases, these families are so poor that every member of their family needs to work. It is likely that these families cannot afford the cost of education for their children. Even when schooling is ostensibly[3] 'free' studies have shown that parents incur other direct costs such as activity fees, uniforms, paper and pens, text books, transport, lunches and others which often result in the exclusion of poor children from school. I am stating the obvious to say that child labour creates a trade-off between labour and education. However, if their choice is either starving or going to school, isn't survival the obvious choice?

[1]pervasive – widespread
[2]impoverished – poor
[3]ostensibly – apparently

Extract **2**

Extract from *The American Frugal Housewife* by Lydia Child

In this country, we are apt to let children romp away their existence, till they get to be thirteen or fourteen. This is not well. It is not well for the purses and patience of parents; and it has a still worse effect on the morals and habits of the children. 'Begin early' is the
5   great maxim for everything in education. A child of six years old can be made useful; and should be taught to consider every day lost in which some little thing has not been done to assist others.

Children can very early be taught to take all the care of their own clothes.

10   They can knit garters, suspenders, and stockings; they can make patchwork and braid straw; they can make mats for the table, and mats for the floor; they can weed the garden, and pick cranberries from the meadow, to be carried to market.

Provided brothers and sisters go together, and are not allowed to
15   go with bad children, it is a great deal better for the boys and girls on a farm to be picking blackberries at six cents a quart, than to be wearing out their clothes in useless play. They enjoy themselves just as well; and they are earning something to buy clothes, at the same time they are tearing them.

Tip In an exam situation, if you choose to use a table to compare two writers' attitudes, you should use key words as notes to save time. Then you can use these as prompts as you write up your response. A quickly sketched table is only a plan to help you assemble your thoughts. You need full sentences in your proper answer to give the detail required by the question.

In Activity 2, question 7 you might have written down a sentence like 'Both texts are in favour of child labour.' This is true but oversimplifies the actual views of the texts. When you put together your answer from your table of ideas, you need to make sure that you use specific details from the texts. The top band in the mark scheme asks you to 'make comparisons that are sustained and detailed'. To do this you need to:

- be as specific as possible about what the writers actually say
- use brief quotations to support your ideas
- comment on whether the views are exactly the same, partly similar or totally different.

There are quite a few ideas in the extracts which can be linked together. Some are more obvious than others. The highlighting in the table below shows where both writers consider a topic. Full sentences are used here so the ideas are clear.

Activity 3

Use your notes on the similarities and differences to add some details to the opening sentence: 'Both texts are in favour of child labour.' You might go on to support this point with an explanation like this: 'For example, Extracts 1 and 2 both deal with the idea that child labour supports families who need the money.' You could then add a quotation from each extract to evidence the point.

Activity 4

Look carefully at the ideas in the table.

1. Add to your list any ideas from the table below that you might have missed.

2. Now look at the ideas which have been linked together by colour. With a partner talk through the link that has been made.
   - Look at words which are similar to help you, for example, 'play' and 'romp' (which means 'to play about together in a rough and lively way').
   - Are there any links you are not sure about? Consult another pair or ask your teacher.

3. Now take each colour/topic in turn. Decide on whether the writers give a wholly or partly similar view on the topic or whether they give a totally different view.

Extract 1	Extract 2
1A. Children should be in school (not working).	2A. It is bad that children can 'romp away their existence' till age 13 or 14 for parents in terms of their patience and their money.
1B. Children should be playing with their friends (not working).	2B. Not working has a bad effect on children's morals and habits.
1C. Child labour happens because poor families depend on the income.	2C. Children as young as six can be 'useful'.
1D. Poor families cannot afford the associated costs of education so children are excluded from school.	2G. Children will ruin clothes during 'useless play' – better to pick blackberries and earn money at the same time as tearing their clothes.
	2F. They can do a variety of jobs.
1E. Child labour is a trade-off: not starving and working is a better option for survival than education.	2D. Children should be taught that not helping others is a waste of a day.
	2E. Children should be taught to take care of their own clothes.

Understanding the views of each writer is the first main task to occupy your time in an exam. You want to make sure that you are representing the views accurately and not misreading anything because you've missed key words or not understood what is being said. You might also consider whether you are convinced by the views presented and why. The student responses which follow will help you to consider how these elements work together in an answer.

Activity 5

Remind yourself of the question you are considering:

> Both writers give their views on child labour. Compare the following:
>
> - the writers' attitudes to child labour
> - how they get across their arguments. **[10]**

The two student responses on page 107 consider how each writer gives their views on how child labour is related to family income or saving money. Read the answers carefully and discuss the following with a partner:

1. How accurately are the views from the texts represented?
2. How are quotations used?
3. Do the students explain the ideas in the text clearly?
4. What comparative words are used to link ideas?
5. How do the students communicate the intended reader or purpose of the texts?
6. Do the students consider how the writers' views are put across?
7. Do the students consider whether the writers' ideas are convincing?

Activity 6

Now look at the mark scheme below. One of the responses might have achieved a mark of 3–4 and the other might have achieved a mark of 9–10.

1. Decide which response you think achieved which mark and give reasons for your answer.
2. What targets would you give to the writer of the response which achieved a mark of 3–4?

Marks	Criteria
0	• Nothing worthy of credit
1–2	• Identifies basic similarities and/or differences
3–4	• Identifies and gives a straightforward description of some of the main similarities and differences
5–6	• Identifies similarities and differences and makes some comparisons, commenting on how they are conveyed
7–8	• Makes detailed comparisons, with valid comments on how they are conveyed
9–10	• Makes comparisons that are sustained and detailed, showing clear understanding of how they are conveyed

Student 1

Both texts are in favour of child labour as a way of supporting the family income. However, Extract 1 makes this more explicit than Extract 2 by saying 'every' family member must work as the family 'depend' on the income. This suggests there is no way out for the children. The other option is to 'starve', an alternative which no reader would see as a positive solution. Although the writer acknowledges that children 'should' be in school or playing with their friends, they present the practical reality of life in developing countries where child labour is the only way to avoid starvation in a less than 'perfect' world. Therefore, the reader sympathizes with the view presented as the writer seems reluctant to support children working but sees it as a necessity. Extract 2 takes a different approach and does not suggest that child labour is essential to the family's survival but seems to assume that the reader wants to save money and that children can be 'useful' in this. The book the extract is taken from, 'The Frugal American Housewife', appears to have the purpose of advising the reader how to save money with specific methods. 'Frugal' means 'careful and economical with money'. The example of children earning money while picking blackberries is seen as better than other 'useless play' as it provides a means of income to mend clothes which they could have torn without earning money at the same time.

Student 2

Both texts talk about children earning money. Extract 1 says, 'Child labour continues for the simple reason that impoverished households who cannot meet their basic needs may depend on the income of their children for survival.' This shows that the money the children earn is needed by the families. In the same way, Extract 2 says, 'They enjoy themselves just as well; and they are earning something to buy clothes, at the same time they are tearing them.' The children earn money with the blackberries they pick.

Activity 7

Now use what you've learned to write up the other three topics which are listed in the comparison table in Activity 4: play, helping others, education/teaching.

- Choose the topic you feel most able to explain and start there.

- Keep the question and mark scheme close to hand to use as prompts for your writing.

- Write in clear sentences and remember to follow PEE – point, evidence, exploration.

14 Comparing how writers convey their views

Assessment Objective

- **AO3**
  - 1c Compare writers' ideas, as well as how these are conveyed, across two or more texts.
  - 1d Compare writers' perspectives, as well as how these are conveyed, across two or more texts.

There are lots of synonyms for the word 'convey' such as 'communicate', 'present', 'suggest', 'express', 'put across', and they all mean the same thing for you in the exam. You should compare the methods the writer has used. This can be a tricky business when you're considering two writers at once. It's not enough to spot methods like similes or statistics. You must explain the way the method appeals to the intended reader or fulfils the text's purpose. In this unit you are going to focus on a pair of texts which both consider how men first experienced magic that would change them into magicians.

The extracts you compare in the exam will be from different time periods and might be from different genres. These factors impact on the methods used by their writers. There is no checklist you can work through: the methods you select will depend on what the writer has chosen to put in. You might be able to comment on similarities and differences in: tone of voice (sarcastic, sympathetic, angry); how they treat the audience (instruct, guide, inform); word choices (simple, metaphorical, scientific); formality or use of humour; use of facts or specific examples. However, there are many more methods a writer can use.

Activity 1

Consider the following question:

> Both extracts explain how the men first encounter magic and how magic makes them feel. Compare:
>
> - the way they first encounter magic
> - how their experiences and feelings are put across. **[10]**

Tip Remember that a text can show you feelings explicitly by using words like 'loved' or 'fascinated', or they can make you infer a deeper meaning by careful word choices. For example, 'I devoured the mysterious pages' carries the sense of reading quickly or greedily, and shows the man's excitement and curiosity.

Extract 1 is taken from a newspaper article in which the 21st-century illusionist Dynamo comments on how he was bullied as a child and how he found magic. Extract 2 was written by Jean Eugène Robert-Houdin in the mid-19th century and explains how he went to buy a book on clockmaking but the bookseller mistakenly gave him a book called *Scientific Amusements*.

1. Track through each extract and list the experiences the men describe.

2. Select quotations to highlight the methods used to show these experiences. You might choose to present your ideas in a table. An example for Extract 1 is given below.

Experiences and feelings	Quotation which highlights method
Great-grandfather is given the role of saviour by introducing Dynamo to magic and providing a way for him to escape from the bullies.	Positive language used to describe Grandpa: 'role model and saviour'; and solution he provides to problem: 'escape route'

Extract 1

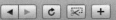

Wimp who walks on water: Bullied at school for being puny, he's the council house boy who's become our most mesmerising magician

Jane Fryer

'To start with it was mostly verbal bullying, but then they started stealing my money and putting me in wheelie bins and throwing me down the hill.'

It was his great-grandfather Kenneth Walsh — the role model and saviour he called Grandpa — who provided the escape route.

'He showed me some magic tricks that he'd used in World War II to supplement his bar money — any way you can make money in a dodgy fashion in a bar, he knew how.'

He also taught Steven a concentration technique that — don't ask how — made his body impossible to lift so that however much they huffed and puffed, the bullies couldn't shift his slight frame any more. (He used the same trick on boxer David Haye.)

'These guys weren't the smartest cookies, and once I started doing a few things they didn't understand, they were freaked out and spread rumours that I had demon powers.

'That stopped people picking on me, but it also isolated me. People didn't want to be around me. But I loved magic and it made my mum smile, and that meant everything. So I spent a lot of time in my bedroom practising.'

 6 4 0

Extract 2

Extract from *Self-Training* by Jean Eugène Robert-Houdin

I opened it impatiently, and, on running through the table of contents, my surprise was doubled on reading these strange phrases: The way of performing tricks with the cards—How to guess a person's thoughts—To cut off a pigeon's head, to restore it to life, etc., etc.

5   The bookseller had made a mistake. [...] Fascinated, however, by the announcement of such marvels, I devoured the mysterious pages, and the further my reading advanced, the more I saw laid bare before me the secrets of an art for which I was unconsciously predestined[1].

I fear I shall be accused of exaggeration, or at
10   least not be understood by many of my readers, when I say that this discovery caused me the greatest joy I had ever experienced. At this moment a secret presentiment[2] warned me that success, perhaps glory, would one day accrue[3].

[1]predestine – to determine an outcome in advance
[2]presentiment – a feeling or foreboding about the future
[3]accrue – to accumulate

Once you've got ideas from both texts you need to link points by topic or methods used by the writers. A mixture of these approaches has been taken in the table below which shows the links in underlined text. For example, both texts deal with the consequences of learning magic by commenting on the future, both use specific examples of tricks, and both use the first person, but in Extract 1 this is only in the direct speech. You should not write a plan in the exam with as much detail as this. The references to specialist terms and quotations here are to support your understanding of the thought processes behind the links; in the exam your annotations would suffice as prompts.

Dynamo	Houdin
Initial difficult situation: examples of bullying given 'verbal', 'stealing' and physical torment. Third person – distanced from victim of bullying	Finds book by chance: 'The bookseller had made a mistake.' First person throughout – we track his experiences first hand
Promise of way out of bullying: 'escape route'	Thinking of future success: 'predestined', 'presentiment', 'success, perhaps glory'
Admiration for Grandpa: 'role model and saviour'. General focus on topic first: 'some magic tricks' – their success suggested as Grandpa made money but also strangeness suggested: 'dodgy fashion' (direct speech)	Initial positive emotion: excitement – adverb 'impatiently' used to describe way he opens book, speed of verb 'running' through contents, greedily consumes the material: 'devoured'
Specific example of tricks which Grandpa shows him: 'concentration technique'. Sense of mystery in aside: 'don't ask how'	Finding out a secret conveyed by specific examples taken from book 'to restore to life'; words associated with magic and mystery: 'fascinated', 'strange', 'marvels', 'mysterious', 'secrets', 'art', 'discovery'
Reader feels joy – the bullies 'stopped picking on' D but also sadness that he is 'isolated'. D gives sense of his joy: 'I loved magic'	Joy shown by superlative – 'greatest joy I had ever experienced'

Activity 2

Use the notes in the table on page 110 to give a full answer to the question:

> Both extracts explain how the men first encounter magic and how magic makes them feel. Compare:
> - the way they first encounter magic
> - how their experiences and feelings are put across. **[10]**

> **Tip** Always make sure you say which text you get your ideas from, otherwise you aren't making clear comparisons.

Remember to do the following:

- Give an overview of the main similarities/differences in their experiences.
- Use short precise quotations like the ones in the table to support your ideas.
- Explain clearly the methods each writer uses by focusing on what they show/mean. Then explore the impact they might have on how a reader views the experience or feelings.
- Explicitly state if a similar or different method is used. Give a reason why.
- Use comparative vocabulary to link ideas.
- Consider which text you found more interesting and why.

Progress check

Look back at the tips list in Activity 2 and the mark scheme on page 106. Swap your work with a partner and use the criteria to mark their response.

1. Highlight two examples of success in the work.
2. Star any ideas which you had not thought of.
3. Give a target for improvement.
4. When you get your own work back, improve it by acting on the target or including any ideas from your partner's work.

15 Comparing purpose and audience

Assessment Objective

- **AO3**
  – Compare writers' ideas and perspectives, as well as how these are conveyed, across two or more texts.

In this unit you will revise how the purpose and audience of a text can shape the kinds of language used within it. Secondly, you will revise how to make comments on the effectiveness or appeal of a text. You will combine both of these elements to compare two texts on police constables.

The texts which follow are both about the duties of a police officer or police constable. The first text, 'Police officer: Job description', is from Prospects, a Careers Advisory website. The second, 'Instructions for Constables', is taken from a book called *The Constables Pocket Companion and Guide*, given to police constables in 1830.

The type of exam question you could be asked about these two texts is:

> Compare and contrast the duties of police officers and how they are presented in these texts.
>
> Comment on:
>
> - what duties the police officers have
> - the words and phrases used. **[10]**

Activity 1

Read both texts carefully. Make notes on the following questions (you might like to set your ideas out in a table):

1. What is the purpose of each text? What clues are there from the ideas included and the language choices?

2. Who is the intended audience for each text? What clues do you get from the ideas included or the tone?

3. What are the duties given in each extract? How are they similar and different? Why might this be? How might the differences be shaped by the time in which the texts were written?

Extract 1

Police officer: Job description

Police officers work in partnership with the communities they serve to maintain law and order, protect members of the public and their property, prevent crime, reduce the fear of crime and improve the quality of life for all citizens. They use a wide range of technology to protect individuals, identify the perpetrators of crime and ensure successful prosecutions against those who break the law.

Key priorities for the 45 police forces in the UK include maintaining public order through combating organised crime, countering the threat of terrorism, and acting against antisocial behaviour.

Police officers work closely with members of the criminal justice system, social workers, schools, local businesses, health trusts, housing authorities, town planners and community groups to provide advice, education and assistance to those who want to reduce crime or have been affected by crime.

Extract 2

Extract from *The Constables Pocket Companion and Guide*

In order to impress constables with the nature and importance of their office, and to direct their attention to a diligent discharge of their several and important duties, it is usual for the justices of peace to issue printed instructions to the constable of each parish within their jurisdiction, in the following form:

5 To Mr. _____ constable of the parish of _____, in the county of _____

It is your duty, as constable, to visit alehouses frequently, at times when you are *not* expected; and to see that no irregularities are permitted.

10 To give notice to magistrates of such persons as keep alehouses without a license.

To prevent drunkenness, by giving notice of such as are guilty of it.

To prevent gaming, and to give notice to justices of those
15 who keep houses in which gaming at any time is permitted.

To seize any tables or implements for gaming, used at fairs or other public meetings.

To prevent abuses of the Lord's Day, commonly called
20 Sunday, such as tippling in alehouses during divine service, using dogs, guns, snares, nets, or other engines for killing or destroying game, using games or pastimes, following worldly callings, or travelling with wagons, vans, or other carriages; and driving cattle.

PEG and BOBBY.

A Burlesque Parody, on that Tender Song call'd Love & Glory. ___ *Written & Sung by Ga*

Young Bobby was as blythe a youth, | Fair Peg, disguis'd, and void of fear, | At length, attack'd by runne
As ever grac'd an attic story, | Join'd Bobby's hand, so fam'd in story, | Peg fell, besmear'd with w
And Peg, so fair, had ne'er a tooth; | And nightly robb'd each trav'ler dear, | And Bob was hung on Tyb
She mended chains, He sought for Glory. | She for pure Love, and He for Glory. | She died for Love, and

Activity 2

Below are a series of language techniques used in one or both of the texts on page 113.

1. Look at each technique carefully and decide which text it is used in. Lots of them are used in both so you will have a number of similarities to comment on.

2. Give a reason why the technique is used for the intended audience.

3. Decide how the technique relates to the purpose of the text.

> **Tip** Even if the technique is used in both texts it might not be used in the same way. For example, lists are used throughout both texts but for different purposes. Can you explain how they function?

Audience:

- Third-person address: 'Police officers work', 'They use'
- Use of a specific name and location
- Second-person direct address: 'your duty'

Purpose:

- Verbs: 'to protect', 'to visit alehouses', maybe in a list
- Words to do with crime: 'perpetrators', 'prosecutions', 'terrorism', 'irregularities', 'magistrates', 'drunkenness'
- Words to do with other roles or groups in the community: 'social workers', 'schools', 'local businesses'
- Words to do with Christianity: 'the Lord's Day', 'Sunday', 'divine service'
- Lists of equipment, activities, people or organizations

Activity 3

One way to organize your answer to the exam question is to focus on a language feature at the beginning of a paragraph and relate it to the audience and purpose of the text. Complete each of the paragraph starters below with quotations from each text and a comment on purpose and audience which explains why the language technique has been used.

- Both texts use lists of verbs to show the duties expected of a police constable.
- Whereas the first text uses a third-person address throughout, the second text uses first person in the opening of the letter and second person when listing the duties of the police officer.
- Both texts use words associated with crime, but the words of Extract 1 cover a wider variety of crimes whereas Extract 2 seems mainly focused around crimes of the alehouses.

Activity 4

Another way to structure your answer can be to link a point about duties to a language feature which shows this. Read the example student response below which starts off in this way. Continue it by making a point about how the idea is presented in Extract 2. Then link this to the purpose and audience of the text.

The wider role of the police constable is considered in Extract 1, whereas in Extract 2 his role seems purely for the prevention and detection of crime. Extract 1 lists nouns, 'advice, education and assistance', which are all positive and might attract people to the role who want to do good in the community. This fits with the purpose as it informs those who are considering joining the police force about all of the different types of work involved. In contrast, Extract 2 seems largely focused on catching criminal activity and informing the authorities of it. This is shown...

Activity 5

Now use all your ideas and notes to write up a full answer to this question. Remember to compare *both* the duties which are mentioned *and* the words/phrases used.

Refer back to the mark scheme on page 106 and the advice given in Activity 2, opposite, to help guide your answer.

Compare and contrast the duties of police officers and how they are presented in these texts.

Comment on:

- what duties the police officers have
- the words and phrases used. [10]

(16) Responding to research

Assessment Objective

- **AO4**
  – Evaluate texts critically and support this with appropriate textual references.

To give a personal or critical response you need to use your skills of evaluation. You might be asked 'What do you think and feel about…?' or 'How do you react to…?' This could be a topic, person or idea. You should make your judgement and explain how the ideas or words used in the text make you think or feel a certain way. A personal response focuses on the reader and the effect a text has on the way you think or feel towards the content presented. You might reflect on whether your first impressions changed as you read deeper into the text and should try to give an overview of your reaction. A critical response might be judging the effectiveness of the writer's arguments or their word choices. For example, do they give a balanced or one-sided view? Is their argument based on factual evidence, examples and research or does it make an emotive issue sensational by using inflammatory opinions? Does the writer deliberately try to persuade you using heavy-handed tactics or do they let the information stand for you to make a judgement? You will explore both of these methods in the next few units.

Activity 1

What is your response to the headline of the article opposite: 'Little liars grow up to be great leaders'?

1. Why do you think the writer has started their article with a statement like this?

2. What words or methods are important here? Explain what they mean.

3. What kinds of feelings does the headline create?

Activity 2

The article starts off in a deliberately provocative way. Lying goes against everyday morals and acceptable behaviour and isn't a quality we'd want in a 'leader'. The writer highlights this using the alliterative linking of the seemingly negative label 'liar' and the more positive 'leader'. Pairing opposites of size such as 'little' and 'great' further emphasizes this contrast and enforces the writer's argument that lying in young children signifies intelligence, not negative behaviour.

1. Read the rest of the article and write down other contrasts.

2. What do you think and feel about these contrasts?

3. Why has the writer included them? How do they support the main argument?

Little liars grow up to be great leaders

Researchers have found that the ability to tell fibs at the age of two is a sign of a fast-developing brain and means children are more likely to have successful lives.

A team of Canadian academics[1] have found that the more plausible the lie, the more quick-witted they will be in later years and the better their ability to think on their feet.

'Parents should not be alarmed if their child tells a fib,' said Dr Kang Lee, director of the Institute of Child Study at Toronto University who carried out the research. 'Almost all children lie. Those who have better cognitive[2] development lie better because they can cover up their tracks. They may make bankers in later life.'

Lying involves multiple brain processes, such as integrating sources of information and manipulating the data to their advantage. It is linked to the development of brain regions that allow executive functioning[3] and use higher order thinking and reasoning.

Dr Lee and his team tested 1,200 children aged two to 16 years old. They found at the age of two, 20 per cent of children will lie. This rises to 50 per cent by three and almost 90 per cent at four. The most deceitful age, they discovered, was 12, when almost every child tells lies.

Researchers say there is no link between telling fibs in childhood and any tendency to cheat in exams or to become a fraudster[4] later in life.

[1]academics – people with great knowledge of a particular subject, often working in a university or college
[2]cognitive – to do with knowledge or understanding
[3]executive functioning – a set of mental skills, such as planning, problem solving and verbal reasoning, that work together to help a person achieve goals
[4]fraudster – someone who makes gain, usually financial, by deceiving people

Activity 3

Key to evaluating an argument is judging how realistic or persuasive the claims are. The argument above uses research throughout.

1. Count how many times the researcher or research is mentioned in the article.

2. Discuss with a partner the effect of using research in this way.

3. We can probably never be certain that research is totally trustworthy but how might research be presented to make it seem more reliable?

Activity 4

Gather together your ideas. Spend 10 minutes answering this exam-style question:

> What do you think and feel about the argument that little liars grow up to be great leaders? You should comment on:
>
> • what is said
>
> • how it is said. **[10]**

17 Thinking around the topic to give a persuasive evaluation

Assessment Objective

- **AO4**
  – Evaluate texts critically and support this with appropriate textual references.

Sometimes the exam topic will be something you will have an opinion on. Be aware that having a pre-formed opinion will change the way you respond to the material in the exam text. You might automatically come up with a counterargument or suggest material that is not covered. This does not put you at an advantage to someone who has not considered the ideas before. You need to 'show engagement and involvement' with the text used in the exam to achieve top marks. The exam text must be the source of your information rather than your own ideas.

The impact of technology on our daily lives is a topic you might have considered before and is the focus of Joe Mayes' article 'Generation text gets more screen time than sleep'. You are going to be guided through how to answer the following exam-style question:

> How do you react to the ideas about technology use in this article? You should comment on what is said and how it is said. **[10]**

Activity 1

You already know that the title or headline of a text often signals the main topic or viewpoint. Look carefully at this headline: 'Generation text gets more screen time than sleep'. Discuss with a partner how you react to the information here:

1. What information is given?
2. Write the questions a reader might ask to judge the topic; for example: 'Is it a good thing that…?'
3. Write answers to the questions you posed.
4. Is your view mainly positive or negative?

Now read the article opposite.

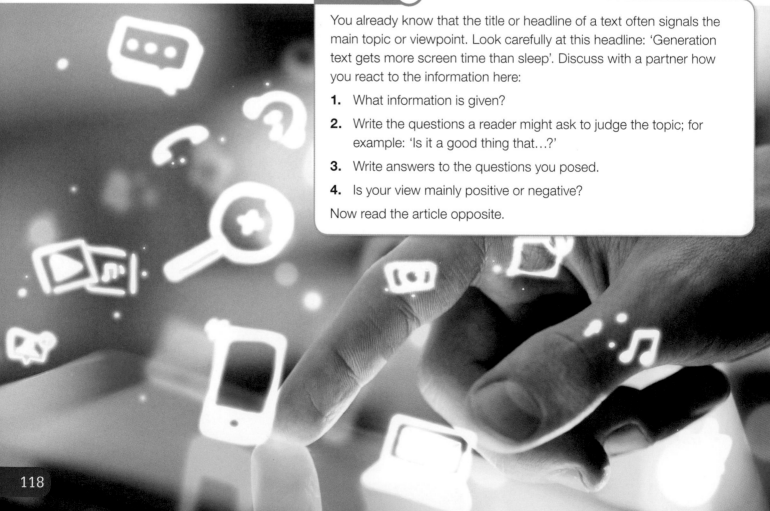

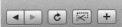

Generation text gets more screen time than sleep

Joe Mayes

Britons now spend more time watching TV, using their mobile and on the computer than they do sleeping, according to new research.

The study, by communications regulator Ofcom, found that the average UK adult uses technology for eight hours and 41 minutes a day, 20 minutes longer than they spend in bed.

The research also found – perhaps worryingly – that six-year-olds have the same understanding of using gadgets such as tablets and mobile phones as 45-year-olds, whilst people were reaching their peak understanding of digital technology at the age of 14 to 15.

Ofcom chief executive Ed Richards said: 'Our research shows that a "millennium generation" is shaping communications habits for the future. While children and teenagers are the most digitally savvy, all age groups are benefiting from new technology.'

 Share

 Tweet

 Email

 Save

Dr Arthur Cassidy, however, a social media psychologist*, expressed concerns about the trends revealed in the report: 'We are increasingly shifting away from human social interactions and this excessive use of technology presents a developmental concern.

'We are now saturated with digital technology and people are becoming psychologically dependent on their smartphones and technology,' he told *The Independent*.

Dr Cassidy linked the findings with increasing instances of internet and social media addiction among young people, associated with problems such as lack of attention, focus and quality sleep.

Other key findings of the Ofcom report include evidence that almost nine in 10 of 16 to 24-year-olds have a smartphone, using them for an average of three hours and 36 minutes per day.

Young people are also increasingly turning away from talking on the phone, with only three per cent of their communications time spent on voice calls.

The overwhelming majority of their time spent communicating (94 per cent) was text-based, such as using social media sites or instant messaging.

Jane Rumble, head of media research and intelligence at Ofcom, said the data led to the 'question whether the millennium generation is losing its voice' or whether children will make voice calls more as they get older.

*psychologist – a specialist or expert in the human mind and how its workings affect behaviour

Activity 2

Consider what you learn about technology from the article on page 119 and whether it supports your first impressions from the headline. Sometimes factual information is presented and sometimes it is the view of an individual.

1. Write the headings <u>Facts</u> and <u>Opinions</u> in your book and list the facts and opinions on technology in the article. If the views are implicit, keep a note of the details which gave you that view.

2. Look through your lists. Identify which facts and opinions seem to be giving a positive view by using 🙂 and a negative view with 🙁. Show those you are unsure about or which could be seen both ways as 😐.

3. How does your view of the topic compare with your first impressions from Activity 1?

If you say whether a viewpoint gives a positive or negative stance, you have already made a judgement about it. One way to give a 'persuasive evaluation of the text and its effects' is to think around the subject and consider alternative viewpoints or responses to the information presented. Look at how this student has tried to do this:

The article begins with factual information which allows the reader their own judgement about an adult spending '20 minutes longer' using technology such as 'watching TV, using their mobile phone and on the computer than they do sleeping'. There aren't any words which suggest it is a good or bad thing. It is possible to respond to this research from Ofcom as showing a worrying state of affairs given that sleep is valuable for health. However, if we take into account that a large number of jobs involve work on a computer then this fact seems to speak more about the important role of technology in our everyday lives.

Activity 3

Go through the facts and opinions you listed in response to Activity 2. Think 'around' the topic and look closely at the way the information is presented to decide whether it is possible to interpret the information as giving a negative or positive view of technology. You should:

- Use the example student response as a guide for your own writing.

- Explain the meaning and effect of any loaded language in your example such as 'worryingly', 'savvy', 'concerns', 'excessive', 'saturated', 'dependent', 'addiction', 'overwhelming'.

- Consider the role of the person giving the information and how trustworthy or knowledgeable they are, for example, 'Dr Arthur Cassidy… a social media psychologist' or 'Jane Rumble, head of media research and intelligence at Ofcom'.

- Write a concluding paragraph showing your overall judgement of the argument.

Activity 4

Evaluate your response using the mark scheme below.

Set yourself a target for improvement and then re-write a section of your answer which will help you to achieve that target.

Marks	Criteria
0	• Nothing worthy of credit
1–2	• Expresses a simple personal opinion with linked basic textual references • May struggle to engage with the text and/or the question
3–4	• Gives a personal opinion supported by straightforward textual references • Shows limited interaction with the writer's views
5–6	• Gives an evaluation of the text and its effects, supported by appropriate textual references • Shows some critical awareness of the writer's views
7–8	• Gives a critical evaluation of the text and its effects, supported by well-selected textual references • Shows critical awareness and clear engagement with the writer's views
9–10	• Gives a persuasive evaluation of the text and its effects, supported by convincing, well-selected examples and purposeful textual references • Shows engagement and involvement, where student takes an overview to make accurate and perceptive comments on the writer's views

(18) Giving an overview

Assessment Objective

● **AO4**
  – Evaluate texts critically and support this with appropriate textual references.

Giving an overview means stepping back from the smaller details in order to summarize. You might signal this in your writing by using phrases such as 'Taking everything into account...' or 'Overall,...' but there is no necessity to do this in order to show an overview. Students often leave an overview to the end of the response. It seems to be easier to give it here as you have spent time delving into the details of the text. It's even better if you can explain how each of the little details supports your main response – a bit like how all the little bones of a fish connect to the spine.

Activity 1

Carla Power starts her article below by posing a question which invites you to evaluate the behaviour of a mother towards one of her sons. She connects with the reader throughout the article by inviting them to consider what they would do and shows her own opinion through her word choices.

Read her article and after each paragraph write down how you feel about the mother, the child and the writer. Record your ideas in a table and give evidence for your ideas.

Paragraph number	Thoughts and feelings about the mother	Thoughts and feelings about the child	Thoughts and feelings about the writer

---

A mother shakes her child in public – do you step in?

Carla Power

The woman pinches his arm and when he cries, she swears and tells him he's bad. What should you do, if anything?

On a packed bus one recent Saturday, I watched an ugly scene unfold. A mother shaking a boy aged perhaps six or seven. Not super-hard, you understand, but borderline rough. Then the boy complained to his mother that she had punched him.

'That wasn't a punch,' she said. 'That was a push.' To drive home the point, she pushed him, right in the centre of his chest. 'This,' – she hit his arm – 'is a punch. I suppose you'll go telling everyone that I've been hitting you now?'

The boy sank to the floor of the bus and started to cry. I stared disapprovingly at the woman but she didn't notice.

'Get up,' the mother said. If he didn't, she warned, she'd pull him up by his ear.

'Why are you so bad?' she kept on. 'None of my other children are bad like you are.'

He started to cry. For three bus-stops, I stood there, like some strap-hanging Hamlet, wondering whether or not to act. To intervene or not to intervene? That is always the question when you see something like this – an incident not violent enough to warrant a panicked call to 999, but disturbing enough to make you very worried.

Activity ②

Look at the repeated ideas in your table, for example you might have focused on the cruelty of the mother and your sympathy for the boy. Draw out an overview of your response by answering these questions:

1. What is your reaction to the mother's behaviour by the end of the article?

2. How do you feel towards the son?

3. How does Power make you question whether 'you [should] step in'?

Activity ③

Now spend 10 minutes writing your response to this exam-style question:

> Power leaves the question 'do you step in?' without an answer. How do you react to her summary that the mother's behaviour is 'disturbing enough to make you worried'? Explore what she says and how she says it. **[10]**

- Link each of the ideas in your table to your main response.

- Refer to evidence to show where your judgement is coming from.

- Offer alternative judgements if possible.

- Explain the meaning and effect of the key words and phrases which you react to.

Progress check

Swap your response to Activity 3 with a partner.

1. Underline their main response or overview.

2. Highlight in one colour any response which was the same as yours.

3. Highlight in another colour any reaction which was different to yours and which was persuasive.

4. Mark their response using the mark scheme on page 121 and give a target for improvement.

5. When you get your work back, act upon the target you've been given.

123

COMPONENT 2

Section B Writing

Introduction to Component 2, Section B Writing

Component 2 at a glance

Component 2
- 60% of total marks for GCSE English Language
- Assessment length: 2 hours
- Section A Reading
- Section B Writing

Section B: Writing
- 30% of total grade
- Complete TWO compulsory transactional writing tasks.
- Spend 30 minutes on each task, including planning and proofreading.

What types of tasks will be in Section B Writing?

In Section B Writing of the Component 2 exam you will be given TWO tasks to complete. You must read both tasks very carefully. They will be based on realistic transactional tasks that you could be given in everyday life. Transactional means 'to do' – an action task with a purpose. Tasks will include: letters, articles, speeches, leaflets, reviews, reports and any other type of 'real life' writing activity you can think of.

In the Writing section of the exam, it is essential that you understand:

- the purpose of your writing

- the audience you are writing to

- the format for the type of writing you have been asked to complete.

You must read the titles very closely to help you understand the purpose, audience and format.

What is covered in this chapter?

This chapter will help you to prepare for the Writing section of the Component 2 exam. You will have the opportunity to think about the following:

- the different types of tasks you may be asked to complete
- how to plan your writing, adapting it for purpose and audience
- a range of different types of formats
- how to develop your writing
- ways to interest your reader/fulfil the purpose of the task
- how to use language effectively
- how to conclude or end a piece of writing
- how to proofread your work.

Assessment Objectives

Section B: Writing of the Component 2 exam will test your abilities in the following assessment objectives (AOs):

AO5 Communicate clearly, effectively and imaginatively, selecting and adapting tone, style and register for different forms, purposes and audiences.

Organize information and ideas, using structural and grammatical features to support coherence and cohesion of texts.

AO6 Candidates must use a range of vocabulary and sentence structures for clarity, purpose and effect, with accurate spelling and punctuation.

How will this chapter help me prepare for the exam?

Each unit of this chapter will guide you through a range of different types of writing and help you revise a variety of useful skills to enable you to write effectively. You will also have the opportunity to focus on techniques that you will find useful for the exam. There will be plenty of different activities to work through, and the chance for you to think about a range of different ideas for your writing. You will be encouraged to consider the different approaches you may wish to take. For example, when writing a review, you may wish to write a review about something you detest.

To help you to understand how to approach the exam, there will be a varied selection of exam-style tasks for you to plan or complete. There will be sample responses for you to read and assess. There will also be some opportunities for you to develop your spelling, punctuation and grammar skills.

You can revise for the Writing section of the Component 2 exam by preparing for the exam-style tasks in this chapter or by completing them in timed conditions. Always revisit your work, not only by proofreading it carefully, but by thinking about how you can improve specific examples of vocabulary and the techniques you use to engage your reader.

Good luck and enjoy writing!

1 Formal letters

Assessment Objective

- **AO5**
  – 1 Communicate clearly, effectively and imaginatively, selecting and adapting tone, style and register for different forms, purposes and audiences.

Several of the types of tasks you may face in your Component 2 Writing exam will require you to write in a formal tone and use formal language. A formal letter is a form of writing that we use when we want to write to an unfamiliar audience. A formal letter is usually an official form of writing. It is important that you understand the conventions of this type of writing to ensure that your audience take you seriously.

Formal letters are produced for a number of reasons. Some people may write a letter of complaint to express their objections about an issue. Formal letters can also be written to persuade the recipient to do something, for example, to give a refund for faulty goods. Another possible reason for writing a formal letter can be to convey important details or information. When writing a formal letter you must think carefully about your reason for writing, as this will help you to include details that are relevant and appropriate.

Activity 1

1. Make a list of the important things you already know about writing a formal letter.

2. Look at the features of a formal letter below. You should always structure a letter correctly as it gives the right formal impression about you. Read the features carefully and work out the order in which you would expect to see these on a page. Use the information to help you to draw a template for a formal letter.

A Address of recipient
B Detailed paragraphs with key ideas/development of key ideas
C Dear Sir or Madam,
D Yours faithfully,
E Introductory paragraph stating the reasons for the letter
F Concluding paragraph stating next steps
G Address of sender
H Date

Tip If you know the name of the person you are writing to, i.e. Mr Jones, you will need to close your letter with: 'Yours sincerely'.

Activity 2

Read the following exam-style task:

> The governors at your school or college have decided to donate ten laptops to ten of their lucky students. All students have been asked to write a letter to the school governors explaining why they need a laptop and persuading the governors to choose them to have one of the laptops. **Write your letter**. **[20]**

Annotate the exam-style task by completing the following activities. In an exam you may also wish to highlight or underline the key words or phrases as you work through the task.

1. Underline the word or phrase that tells you who you are writing to (the audience).

2. Underline any phrases that help you understand why you are writing the letter (the purpose).

Very few students are able to write a convincing and coherent letter without spending a couple of minutes thinking about or planning what they would like to include. Throughout this unit you will have the opportunity to experiment with a range of different planning techniques. Try them all and see which one works best for you.

Activity 3

The two spider diagrams below have been set up as a starting point to the exam-style task from Activity 2. A student has read the task and jotted down some of their immediate reactions.

1. Copy these spider diagrams and add any other ideas you might have to them.

2. Decide which ideas are similar and could fit together in a paragraph; create two or three paragraph groups.

3. Write a draft of each of your paragraphs.

What sets me apart from my peers?

Why am I a worthy student?

How will I persuade them to give me a laptop?

What have I done at school to deserve it?

Can I use it to bring any value to the school?

Have I got one already?

Why will it help me and my studies?

Why do I want a laptop?

What will I use it for at school/college?

What will I use it for at home?

Key term

Chronologically: arranged in the order in which things occurred

Activity 4

Look at the response below. This student has produced a plan to help them write their letter. The information they plan to include is appropriate and will enable them to write a detailed letter. Go through the plan with a partner and number each section so the student can write their response **chronologically**. Try to explain why the information should go in the order you have suggested.

A Benefits in school — upload homework, print documents, type up notes in lessons or revision classes

B Other reasons why I am deserving — attendance, behaviour, prefect, school council

C Brief explanation to outline why I am writing — want a laptop

D Benefits at home — complete online homework/classwork, email teachers, complete research

E Personal situation — using old borrowed laptop — slow, breaks down, unreliable

The opening paragraph of a formal letter should clarify exactly why you are writing the letter. The recipient of your letter should also be in no doubt as to what your letter aims to achieve.

Activity 5

Several students have written a letter of complaint. Their introductions have been included below. Your task is to work out exactly what they were writing about.

Copy and complete the following table of questions about each of the sample answers. You could work independently or with a partner to discuss each sample and see if you can agree on answers to the questions.

	Student 1	Student 2	Student 3
Who are they writing to?			
Why are they writing?			
What do they hope to achieve?			

Student 1

I am writing to you as I was appalled by your services last weekend. Your staff are rude, your facilities are disgusting and I was very annoyed when I saw the mess outside. Your negligence makes me sick.

Tip If you can't answer the questions in the table, then the opening paragraph is not sufficiently clear.

Student 2

Last weekend my family and I visited your theme park. While the awful weather did not dampen our spirits, the appalling state of the park quite frankly ruined our day. We would like a full refund and a guarantee that further action will be taken.

Student 3

I am a 16-year-old customer of yours who is fed up. I am writing to you as I'd like my money back. I want every single penny or I will take further action.

Key terms

Clearly: a point made that is easy to understand

Effectively: a point made that achieves what you want it to do – it has an effect

Convincing: to make someone feel certain that something is true

Topic sentence: the key sentence that explains what a paragraph is about

Once you have decided what you are going to include in your formal letter, you need to consider how you will make it sound convincing so that a reader will do what you ask. To achieve this you will need to write **clearly** and **effectively**.

Activity 6

Look at the paragraph below which has been taken from another student's letter. The student was applying to win one of the free school laptops from Activity 2 on page 127. A teacher has underlined any sentences that are unclear. They have also highlighted sections where they feel the student could be more effective or, in this case, persuasive.

1. The student was trying to persuade the school governors that a laptop could be useful at home. With a partner, make a list of any other **convincing** reasons that would be more persuasive.

2. Look at the list you have made and highlight three or four key uses of the laptop.

3. Look at your highlighted list and see if you can add any further details or explanations for each of these.

4. Remind yourself of the definition of a **topic sentence**. Write down the topic sentence that you would use to introduce the paragraph below.

5. Rewrite the paragraph with your own reasons and details. Remember to focus on trying to convince the reader that you would be a worthy winner.

I have wanted a laptop of my own for quite a while now and this is a decent chance for me to accumulate one. I think a free laptop would be fairly useful because we only have two computers at home and my mum usually uses one of them doing her job at home. My brother and me ended up fighting over the other computer, which isn't fair on anyone. My dad has his own laptop so it does not really bother him but we are unable to use it as he works from a secure network. My brother is two years older than me and he'd like to win a laptop too so I have told him to write a letter as well. I would spend about half an hour after school every day doing my homework on the laptop and the rest of the time I'd either be surfing the internet, chatting to friends online or playing games. As you can see the laptop would be well used for many an hours a day.

Teacher's comment

You have a few sensible ideas but they are presented factually rather than persuasively. How can you make it seem like you desperately need the computer? Your use of the computer at home (surfing, chatting, etc.) is not particularly persuasive. Your language is straightforward; can you improve any of the words you have selected?

Activity

Read the following exam-style task:

> The local residents near your school have been complaining about student behaviour. To stop these concerns the council plans to introduce 'teen-free' zones in your local area. These will include: all local shops, all supermarkets, school facilities after 4pm and any local housing areas within a one mile radius of the school.
>
> You feel strongly about this proposal and decide to write a letter giving your views. **[20]**

Use the skills you have been working on during this unit to:

- Annotate the exam-style task, working out the audience and the purpose for your writing.

- Produce a spider diagram of what you would like to include.

- Number the ideas on your spider diagram so you can work out the sequence for your ideas.

- Produce a focused introduction.

- Use topic sentences to introduce the main ideas in your paragraphs.

Now write your letter.

2 Informal writing

Assessment Objectives

- **AO5**
  – 1 Communicate clearly, effectively and imaginatively, selecting and adapting tone, style and register for different forms, purposes and audiences.
  – 2 Organize information and ideas, using structural and grammatical features to support coherence and cohesion of texts.

- **AO6**
  – Candidates must use a range of vocabulary and sentence structures for clarity, purpose and effect, with accurate spelling and punctuation.

Tip Although you might be asked to write to a friend or relative, it is important that you remember to retain an appropriate level of formality (slang and inappropriate language are not suitable in an exam).

One of the skills you will need to show in your Component 2 Writing exam is writing in an informal style. You don't know exactly what tasks you might face, but you need to practise this form of writing so you can apply it to a variety of tasks. An informal style is used when we want to write to a familiar audience or someone we know very well. An informal letter, for example, is usually written to a family member or a friend to communicate family news, personal information or request support. Some people write an informal letter to give a view or opinion about something, while others may wish to persuade a friend or family member to do something.

Today we use a range of different methods if we want to write to family members or friends, such as emails. The content of emails and letters is often very similar but the structure will vary between these types of writing. Like formal letter writing, understanding the purpose and audience is crucial.

Activity 1

1. Make a list of the important things you already know about writing an informal letter. For example, how will you start and finish your letter?

2. Look at the list of features below that are used in formal letter writing. Which of these would you expect to see in an informal letter? Make a list of the differences between these two writing styles.

1. **Address of sender**

2. **Address of recipient**

3. **Date**

4. **Dear Sir or Madam,**

5. **Introductory paragraph stating the reasons for the letter**

6. **Detailed paragraphs with key ideas/ development of key ideas**

7. **Concluding paragraph stating next steps**

8. **Yours faithfully,**

Activity 2

Look at this exam-style task and complete the activities that follow:

> You have a friend or relative who is planning to raise some money for a charity your family supports. Write a letter giving your support and suggestions. **[20]**

1. Who are you writing to (audience)?
2. Why are you writing the letter (purpose)?
3. What is the format for your writing?

Tip Be careful when opening and closing your letter. The following are all acceptable:
- Dear, Hi, Hello
- Love, From, See you soon.

Activity 3

Before you start writing, you need to consider carefully what ideas you will include. The exam-style task has asked you to do two main things:

- give support
- give suggestions.

Look at the spider diagrams below. Some ideas have been included for you. Copy and complete these by adding your own ideas. Remember you are writing to someone you know well so try to build up a relationship (you may wish to include: shared jokes, reminiscing, specific details).

Giving support
- Praise your friend/relative
- Explain why this is a valuable charity
- Link to family reasons

Giving suggestions
- Suggest ways to raise money
- Give details about other successes
- Suggest people who can help

Activity 4

If you are writing an informal letter or email you might like to open your writing with a general introduction. This is a great opportunity for you to showcase a range of sentence types and build up a rapport with your audience. It also lets you show the examiner that you have a clear friend or relative in mind.

1. Look at the sample student introduction below. Make a list of the different things that the student has done to demonstrate that they know this person well.

2. Go back through the letter. Can you see a range of different sentence types? Why are these effective in this type of writing?

Dear Holly,

How are things in Norfolk? I can't believe it is almost Christmas again and a full 12 months since we last saw you. It has been a pretty hectic year for us. When Pete lost his job in April (after 25 years of service) we weren't sure how we would manage financially or indeed how we would cope spending so much time together – we didn't need to worry (as I'm sure Aunty Bev has told you) as he was offered a new job the following week and has never been happier. Working for Cancer Research UK has been such a rewarding experience for him. When we lost Martin five years ago we couldn't have coped if it hadn't been for the team of nurses, doctors and carers. Now I hear you're planning to raise money for this worthy cause and I couldn't be prouder...

Activity 5

To produce a convincing letter you need to think carefully about how you take the ideas from your plan and turn them into three or four subsequent paragraphs. Look at the plan below and see if you can add specific details to each of these sections.

Support your friend	
Why is this a worthy cause?	What good work will they be helping by raising money for this charity?

What can they do – suggestions	
General ideas on fundraising	Specific ideas on fundraising

What can they do – suggestions	
Other possible ideas	

When writing informally there is a risk that your writing and vocabulary may not seem as impressive as when you write in a formal style. To ensure writing is ambitious and sophisticated, it is essential that the contents of your letter are detailed, fluent and accurate.
To make sure your writing is awarded a top band mark, you can use the following checklist.

✓ Have I fully understood my audience and demonstrated a clear relationship with them?

✓ Have I included a wide range of sentence types and punctuated them accurately?

✓ Have I linked my ideas together carefully to make my writing fluent and organized?

✓ Have I developed my ideas giving a wide range of supporting reasons and details?

Activity

The following paragraph has been taken from a student's letter. Read through the paragraph carefully and then complete the following activities.

1. Based on this section, the student is working in the top bands for writing. Use the Assessment Criteria for Writing on pages 164–165 and see if you can identify the areas in which they have achieved.

2. In their next paragraph, this student plans to give details about specific events that could be held to raise money. Read the paragraph below and see if you can produce their next paragraph using a similar writing style.

We both know that raising money can be very difficult. Jack and his classmates found it virtually impossible to raise the money they needed to fund the school trip to an African school last year. It took a huge amount of perseverance and dedication (especially when their teacher suggested dressing up outside of Toys R Us every weekend for a month)! You need to be realistic about what you can achieve and must write a clear plan of action. Maybe you could start by producing a clear plan of your fundraising events and don't forget to include really precise dates and timescales! Perhaps you could do one fundraiser a week for a whole month. Try to avoid asking the same people for sponsorship and donations (they'll become totally fed up and less charitable)!

Activity 7

Now you are going to bring together all the skills of informal writing which you have been practising to answer the following exam-style task:

> You have a friend or relative who is thinking about taking a gap year. They hope to work in Australia for 12 months. You have decided to write a letter giving your views. **[20]**

Use the skills you have been working on during this unit to:

- Annotate the exam-style task, working out the audience and the purpose for your writing.
- Produce a spider diagram of what you would like to include.
- Number the ideas on your spider diagram so you can work out the sequence for your ideas.
- Produce a focused introduction.
- Use topic sentences to introduce the main ideas in your paragraphs.

Now write your letter.

3 Report writing

Assessment Objectives

- **AO5**
  – 1 Communicate clearly, effectively and imaginatively, selecting and adapting tone, style and register for different forms, purposes and audiences.
  – 2 Organize information and ideas, using structural and grammatical features to support coherence and cohesion of texts.
- **AO6**
  – Candidates must use a range of vocabulary and sentence structures for clarity, purpose and effect, with accurate spelling and punctuation.

One of the types of tasks you may face in your Component 2 Writing exam could ask you to write a report. A report is a style of writing that is usually written formally and follows a formal layout. Reports can be written to a familiar audience, although these are usually people like head teachers, governors, councillors and people in professional positions. Although you may know these people, you will be required to write in a formal and professional manner. The way a report is set out is important as it adds to the formality of the writing.

Reports have an extremely clear purpose, usually to identify a problem or area for improvement. Throughout the report possible outcomes will be discussed and the report will conclude with a series of recommendations or suggestions.

Activity 1

The following are all features of a report. Can you match the feature to the example?

1. **Title – why are you writing the report?**
2. **Recipient – who are you writing to?**
3. **Introduction**
4. **Introduce the problems**
5. **Develop detail about each specific issue**
6. **Offer a range of solutions**
7. **Summarize your recommendations**
8. **Close your report**

A **Overall we need to...**

B **The first issue is the lack of hygiene**

C **For the attention of: Head teacher: J. Smith**

D **I appreciate the time... and hope that...**

E **I have never seen anyone clean the tables**

F **This report is being written because...**

G **To resolve these issues I suggest...**

H **Re: School canteen closure**

Activity 2

Why do we write reports and who do you think you might write one to?

With a partner make a list of the possible reasons for writing a report and make a list of the possible recipients.

Possible reasons for writing a report	Possible recipients

Activity 3

Read the following exam-style task:

> Your school is keen to raise money for extra equipment. Write a report for the parents' association giving information about:
>
> - what the school needs most urgently and why
> - suggestions as to how the money could be raised. **[20]**

1. Read the exam-style task carefully again and annotate it. Make sure you make notes about:
   - the intended audience/recipient
   - the purpose of the report
   - what you will need to include in your answer.

2. Look again at the exam-style task. Spend two or three minutes with a partner to plan the following:

What the school needs most urgently and why	Suggestions as to how the money could be raised

The following will guide you through a series of steps to help you to write your report. Try to remember how structured this process is as it will help you to produce a clear and focused report in the exam if you are asked to write one.

1. Give your report a clear title

2. Make sure it is clear who your report is to

Report to: The Parents' Association ◄ •••••••• This is brief but it makes it clear who the report is being written for.

Re: Extra School Equipment ◄ •••••••• Again, the writer has made the purpose of the report clear for the reader.

3. Writing your introduction

In this section you need to include the following:

- why you are writing the report
- a couple of suggestions of what the school might need and why
- how you have raised money in the past and a couple of suggestions of what might be done.

Spend five minutes making some notes that will help you to complete an introduction.

4. Paragraphs 1 and 2

In the first two paragraphs you need to start to go into more detail about what the school needs and why you need it. You can make up any reasons that you like as long as they are sensible. Good answers might start off by giving a problem in school – they will then suggest a solution and how things might work in the future. You will need at least three or four different suggestions of what the school needs most. For example:

> The number of students going to eat out of school at lunch and break times seems to cause a number of problems. Not only is it dangerous for students to leave the premises and be unsupervised but the school's reputation is at risk if they misbehave or cause problems for the local community. Teachers need to think about why students leave the buildings during these times — students are bored and do not like the school food. I suggest that we completely change the food given to students at lunchtime by... Students have nothing to do at lunchtime so I suggest that the school...

Spend five minutes making some notes that will help you to complete paragraphs 1 and 2.

5. Paragraphs 3 and 4

In this section you need to suggest how the money will be raised. You might like to think about the following:

- How much money does the school need?
- What is the school going to do first?
- How will the school raise the money? (What activities do you propose?)
- Who will be involved?
- What will the priority be?

Good answers will have quite a number of suggestions and will give some reasons as to why these activities have been chosen.

Spend five minutes making some notes that will help you to complete paragraphs 3 and 4.

6. Conclusion/Recommendations

The main reason for writing a report is to make suggestions of what can be done. In your conclusion you need to summarize your ideas and you can even use bullet points to make your ideas really clear. For example:

> Our main priorities are: We will focus on:
> -   •
> -   •
> -   •

You now just need to thank the person who has read your report, and if you want them to follow up any areas you must make that clear. For example:

> We appreciate the time you have taken to read this report and hope we can rely on your support in the coming months to achieve our goals.
>
> The School Council

Activity 4

Using all of the steps on pages 139–141 and the notes you have made, you are going to write the report in exam conditions. Remind yourself of the task:

> Your school is keen to raise money for extra equipment. Write a report for the parents' association giving information about:
>
> • what the school needs most urgently and why
>
> • suggestions as to how the money could be raised. **[20]**

You have 30 minutes to write your report. You should save a few minutes to check your work.

Progress check

1. Cover up the section where you outline your priorities. Swap work with a partner and ask them to read your report and suggest what they think your priorities are.

2. Now ask your partner to highlight any areas where they do not think you explain your ideas carefully.

3. Using the Assessment Criteria for Writing on pages 164–165 see if you can write down which band you feel your partner's work fits into for:
   • communication and organization
   • vocabulary, sentence structure and spelling.

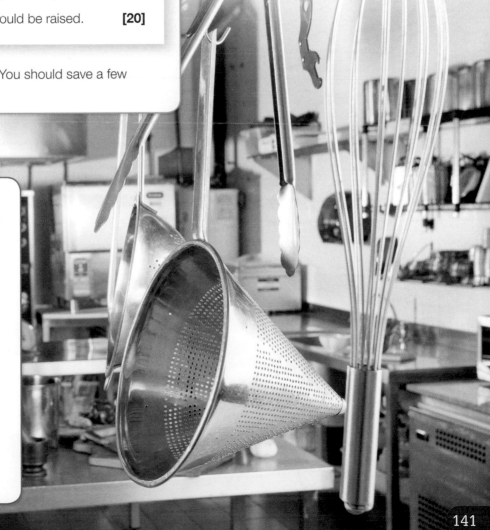

4 Review writing

Assessment Objectives

- **AO5**
  – 1 Communicate clearly, effectively and imaginatively, selecting and adapting tone, style and register for different forms, purposes and audiences.
  – 2 Organize information and ideas, using structural and grammatical features to support coherence and cohesion of texts.
- **AO6**
  – Candidates must use a range of vocabulary and sentence structures for clarity, purpose and effect, with accurate spelling and punctuation.

You could be asked to write a review in your Component 2 Writing exam. You must read these tasks particularly carefully as your intended audience will greatly affect how formal or informal your review can be. A review is a form of writing that we use when we want to evaluate or assess something. When we review something we 'weigh up' what we think about it and share those views and opinions with the reader. The style of the review depends on the audience. If a writer wishes to review something for a teenage audience they may be less formal than if they were writing a review of a new computer software program or building.

Reviews can be written about most things. Anything that can be sold, bought, watched, read or visited can be reviewed. As long as someone has an opinion that they think is worth sharing with an audience, then they can write a review. People read reviews so they can gather other people's opinions about something that they are interested in. Popular websites like Tripadvisor and Argos, for example, include reviews written by other people to help inform their customers who may wish to make a similar purchase. Reviews can be both positive and negative, depending on what the writer feels about the thing they are reviewing.

When writing a review you must think carefully about what you are reviewing and the audience you are writing the review for. This will help you to include details that are relevant and appropriate.

Activity 1

Think about the reviews you have seen or read. In two minutes, make a list of as many different things as you can think of for a writer to review. Why do we review each of these?

What can you review?	Why would you review this?

Activity 2

1. The following spider diagram gives a list of steps for writing a review. Copy the diagram and write a number next to each step to show which step you would take first, second and so on.

2. Now look back at your spider diagram. Can you add any further details or explanations to help you understand each step of the review process?

Write a title including what you are reviewing.

Give a short summary of what you are writing about.

Writing a review

Give clear opinions or critical assessment about what you are reviewing.

Give any final recommendations and suggest who will use or like it.

Activity 3

Look at the book review below.

1. What do you notice about the structure of the review?

2. Can you identify any conventions that a writer uses when writing a review?

Review: *The Hunger Games* by Suzanne Collins

Summary: In the ruins of North America lies the Capitol of Panem. The Capitol controls its 12 surrounding districts by forcing them all to send one boy and one girl, called Tributes, to fight to the death on live TV in the annual Hunger Games.

Review: I've heard about this book for years now, but was never really interested in reading it. At the time, I was reading only urban fantasy or paranormal romance novels and didn't know what to make of the dystopian genre. After seeing the movie trailer for *The Hunger Games*, I was intrigued. I went out and bought the entire series. I am so glad that I read this book, it was way better than I anticipated. The characters and the world-building were exceptionally believable. Katniss and all the other characters in the novel were well developed, and as a reader I felt connected to the characters. Whatever was happening to them in the book, as a reader, I also felt their joy, sadness, and pain.

The pacing of the book was great; it had me constantly turning the pages eager to find out what will happen next. I finished the book in 2 days, would have been sooner if I didn't have school LOL. The book is told from Katniss's point of view; and the majority of the book is full of description rather than the usual dialogue that I read. The ending of the book had a lot of surprises that I wasn't expecting (example: what happened to the dead tributes). Overall, I really enjoyed this book and I would recommend it to anyone who's looking for an action-packed novel. This is my first dystopian book, and surely it will not be my last. I look forward to reading more of Katniss's adventures in the next two books in the trilogy. Like everyone this weekend, I will be watching *The Hunger Games* movie as well!

★★★★☆

 22 15 4

Activity

Read the following exam-style task:

> Imagine you have a relative or friend who is thinking of moving near you. Write a review of your local area, giving your honest opinions. **[20]**

Annotate the exam-style task above by completing the following activities. In an exam you may wish to highlight or underline the key words or phrases as you work through a task.

1. Underline the word or phrase that tells you who you are writing to (the audience).

2. Underline any phrases that help you understand why you are writing the letter (the purpose).

3. Underline any words or phrases that help you to understand what you need to write about.

Activity 5

Using a spider diagram, spend a few minutes jotting down a range of ideas that you might like to include about your local area.

Once you have gathered a range of ideas to include in your review, you need to think carefully about how you review or evaluate the information. Whatever your views about the item or thing you have chosen to review, you need to ensure that a reader will find your information helpful and clear.

Activity 6

Look at the two texts opposite. Two students have written a review about the same place.

1. Read the two reviews carefully. Write down which review you think is better. Why do you think this?

2. Which review is most specific? What has the writer done to achieve this?

3. Who does each review appeal to? Which do you think is most successful in attracting their audience? Explain why.

Student 1

This is a wonderful town which people of all ages love to visit. We have plenty of activities to keep visitors entertained and a wide range of hotels and guest houses should you decide to stay and make a weekend of it.

In the city centre you will find a number of award-winning restaurants to suit every taste bud. There are a number of pubs selling fine wines and traditional ales as well as over a dozen coffee shops. If you like to treat yourself, you should head to some of the less well known places as they tend to be a little cheaper and more hospitable.

Student 2

Krie is a quaint little town situated on the banks of the river Avon. If culture is your thing then it offers a range of garden centres, antique shops and a small museum that celebrates the life of William Shakespeare. However, for those of you looking for a wide range of activities, shops and nightlife, Krie is probably not up your street.

The city centre is full of award-winning restaurants such as Divines, a Mediterranean tapas bar, which won two Michelin stars last year. If fine dining is not your thing, Mezzo is a quirky fast food chain that offers healthy snacks that you can personalize...

One way that a writer can make their opinions clear when writing a review is by using parenthesis. Parenthesis comes from the Greek for 'insertion' and it is a good way of allowing a writer to include additional information, explanation or personal remarks within a sentence. Pairs of brackets, commas and dashes may all be used to signal parenthesis. The choice of which punctuation to use is partly a matter of personal preference and the style of the material. For example:

THE FILM (while packed with A-list actors) has been a sensational flop.

The bracketed information adds subordinate or additional information to the sentence.

Activity

The following sentences have been taken from different reviews. The sentences all contain information that is supplementary. Copy out each sentence and highlight the section of the sentence that gives extra information and insert brackets around the additional information.

1

This film is all about the transformation of clean-cut Anakin Skywalker teen heartthrob Haydn Christenson into the evil Darth Vader.

2

Jennifer Lawrence the highest-grossing action heroine of all time gained international fame in 2012 when she played the leading heroine, Katniss Everdeen, in *The Hunger Games*.

3

X-Men: Days of Future Past combines the best elements of the series and avoids the pitfalls of *X-Men: The Last Stand* to produce a fantastic, fast paced and enthralling film that can be classed as the finest instalment so far.

4

Titanic a three-hour long film marathon is a dazzling achievement in special effects and a triumph in popular art.

5

Batman and Robin may have a star-studded cast but it has been voted one of the worst films of all time receiving three times more votes than any other film.

Activity 8

You have been given the following exam-style task:

> Write a review of your favourite film for a teenage magazine. **[20]**

Use the skills you have been working on during this unit to:

- Choose the film you would like to review – make sure you select something that gives you plenty to write about (both positive and negative).
- Annotate the exam-style task, working out the audience and the purpose for your writing.
- Think about what you will say about the film and produce a spider diagram of what you will include.
- Write down specific details to include (names of actors, songs, director, film budget, etc.).
- Write the opening paragraph of your review and include one example of parenthesis.

5 Writing a speech

Assessment Objectives

- **AO5**
  – 1 Communicate clearly, effectively and imaginatively, selecting and adapting tone, style and register for different forms, purposes and audiences.
  – 2 Organize information and ideas, using structural and grammatical features to support coherence and cohesion of texts.
- **AO6**
  – Candidates must use a range of vocabulary and sentence structures for clarity, purpose and effect, with accurate spelling and punctuation.

One of the types of tasks you may face in your Component 2 Writing exam could ask you to write a speech or talk that you could give to a specific audience. Speeches can be given to a range of different audiences, but understanding the audience is crucial as it will help you select suitable vocabulary and content. Speeches can be given in both formal and informal situations, depending on the topic and the audience.

If you were asked to prepare a speech or talk to give in an assembly at school, it is likely that you would use some prompt or cue cards and that you may choose not to write out the speech in full. In the exam, you would not write notes; instead you must write out the speech exactly as you would say it.

Speeches are given for a number of reasons. Some people may be asked to make a speech to give information or advice to an audience (for example, a speech about safety issues). Speeches can also be made with the purpose of persuading an audience (for example, a speech persuading an audience to support a specific charity) or to get a viewpoint across (for example, a speech about why certain interests are enjoyable).

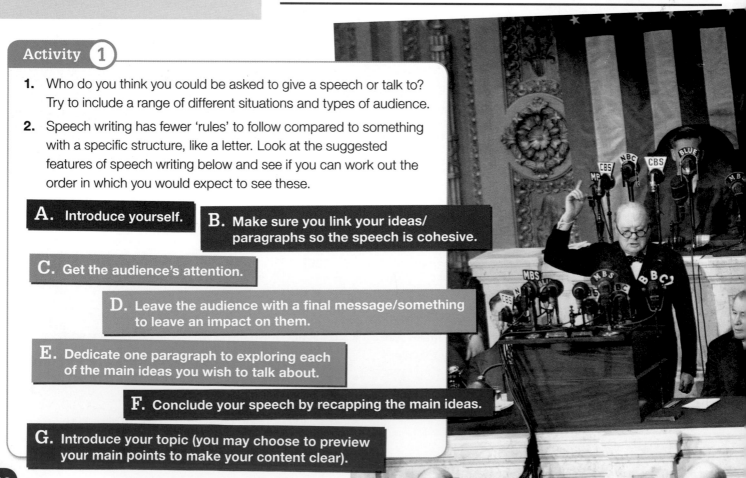

Activity 1

1. Who do you think you could be asked to give a speech or talk to? Try to include a range of different situations and types of audience.

2. Speech writing has fewer 'rules' to follow compared to something with a specific structure, like a letter. Look at the suggested features of speech writing below and see if you can work out the order in which you would expect to see these.

A. Introduce yourself.

B. Make sure you link your ideas/paragraphs so the speech is cohesive.

C. Get the audience's attention.

D. Leave the audience with a final message/something to leave an impact on them.

E. Dedicate one paragraph to exploring each of the main ideas you wish to talk about.

F. Conclude your speech by recapping the main ideas.

G. Introduce your topic (you may choose to preview your main points to make your content clear).

Activity 2

Read the exam-style task below and answer the following questions:

> Your local council has decided to save money by changing school arrangements: school buses will no longer be provided; students will have to supply their own equipment; there will be no school canteen and school trips will cost more.
>
> You have been asked to give a speech to parents at the school to inform them of these changes and to persuade them to take action. [20]

1. Who is the audience for the speech?
2. What is the purpose of this speech?
3. What are your views on this proposal?
4. From whose point of view would you write your speech (teacher, student, parent or councillor)?
5. Are there any techniques you could use in your speech to help persuade the audience to listen to you?

Activity

What makes an effective written speech? Think about the following techniques:

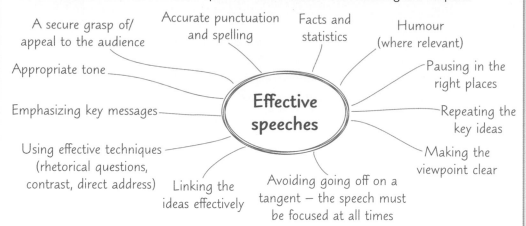

A secure grasp of/appeal to the audience

Accurate punctuation and spelling

Facts and statistics

Humour (where relevant)

Appropriate tone

Emphasizing key messages

Using effective techniques (rhetorical questions, contrast, direct address)

Effective speeches

Pausing in the right places

Repeating the key ideas

Making the viewpoint clear

Linking the ideas effectively

Avoiding going off on a tangent — the speech must be focused at all times

1. Below is a section of a speech written by a student. They were asked to give a speech to parents in response to some negative newspaper articles and comments about teenagers. Read the speech carefully and highlight any effective features that you can spot.

Drunken, disorderly and disrespectful... This is the picture painted of teenagers by many of the daily tabloids every week. 'Teenage crime on the increase... teen pregnancy crisis... hoodies causing havoc...' The headlines paint a particularly grim picture of my classmates and me. But stop, before you take out the Taser guns and phone the police: do you honestly think we all fit this depressing stereotype?

Look around you. 80% of the students in this school gained 5 A*–C grades last year. Isn't that something we can be proud of? Do the headlines mention the 20% increased pass rate at our school? No, they only mention the one idiot who set off a smoke alarm in a local home for the elderly.

Teenagers have it easy according to the older generations. But do any of you really understand the pressures placed upon today's youth? Driven to reach the ever increasing exam statistics, driven to further education due to a lack of funded apprenticeships and driven to despair by competitive parents who feel we ought to be better than ever. Life as a teen is a tough old task. And do we complain? Of course we do, but didn't you?

Parents, ask yourself the following question: when you were our age was it important to wear the right clothes, to meet the right boy or girl and to go to the right social events? Of course it was. Only now it all costs that little bit more. We have to get the right clothes or we're bullied, the right phone or we're bullied and we even have to have the right parents. Yes, you heard me right, the right parents can mean the difference between fitting in and being totally alienated. So next time you think about embarrassing your child in front of their mates, think again. You're not being cool; you're not being tough; you're just signing a 'right to bully' warrant for your dearly beloved child. Being a kid is tough — so come on, parents — help us out.

2. Now look at the Assessment Criteria for Writing on pages 164–165. Can you see any sections of the Assessment Criteria which you feel describe this student's work? Highlight any relevant words and phrases.

This is what the student's teacher wrote about their work:

> Effective grasp of the audience. Some effective techniques have been used to engage the reader. Control is mostly secure. Think about how you could make the structure, development and organization of ideas more effective.

3. Look at the last sentence where the teacher suggests what the student should do to improve. With a partner, go back through the speech and see if you can spot any areas where you could 'make the structure, development and organization of ideas more effective'. The following questions will help you.

Explain some of the reasons behind this statement. Why do older people think they have it easy?

These three points could be separated into three sentences and developed. Are there any other pressures on teenagers?

Why? Can you further develop this statement?

The end of this paragraph is quite effective. Unless you can think of something punchier, leave it as it is.

Teenagers have it easy according to the older generations. But do any of you really understand the pressures placed upon today's youth? Driven to reach the ever increasing exam statistics, driven to further education due to a lack of funded apprenticeships and driven to despair by competitive parents who feel we ought to be better than ever. Life as a teen is a tough old task. And do we complain? Of course we do, but didn't you?

Activity 4

1. What are your views about the teenagers in your school and the local area? Do you think the stereotypical view of teenagers being 'drunken, disorderly and disrespectful' is fair? With a partner or in small groups, make notes on what you think about this topic. The following prompts might help you:

   - Do teenagers cause trouble at your school (give general examples)?
   - Do teenagers cause trouble in your local area (give general examples)?
   - Can you think of any positive things teenagers have done at your school?
   - Can you think of any positive things teenagers have done for your community?

2. Now look at the following exam-style task:

   > Teenagers are stereotyped as 'drunken, disorderly and disrespectful'. Give a speech to teenagers in your school giving your opinions about this view. **[20]**

   Use the following table to plan your views.

Get the audience's attention **Introduce yourself**	
Introduce your speech **Make your viewpoint clear** **Preview your main points**	
Plan 3–4 main ideas that will form the main body (and paragraphs of your speech). These ideas could become topic sentences to introduce each paragraph	
Conclude your speech and recap the main points	
Think of an effective way to leave the audience with a final message or have an impact on them	

   Remind yourself of the effective features of speech writing on page 148. Can you add any of these features to your plan?

Activity 5

1. You are now going to write your speech in sections. Your teacher may give you a specific amount of time (around 6–7 minutes) to write each paragraph/section of your speech. After each paragraph your teacher may ask you to reflect on your work (you may be asked to listen to some of the work being read out, to read a partner's work or to read your own work, etc.). Use this reflection time to read and fine tune your work.

2. When you have completed your speech, use the Assessment Criteria for Writing on pages 164–165 to see if you can place your writing into a band for:

   - communication and organization

   - vocabulary, sentence structure, spelling and punctuation.

6 Articles

Assessment Objectives

- **AO5**
  – 1 Communicate clearly, effectively and imaginatively, selecting and adapting tone, style and register for different forms, purposes and audiences.
  – 2 Organize information and ideas, using structural and grammatical features to support coherence and cohesion of texts.
- **AO6**
  – Candidates must use a range of vocabulary and sentence structures for clarity, purpose and effect, with accurate spelling and punctuation.

We commonly find articles in newspapers or magazines and you may be asked to produce one in your Component 2 Writing exam. If you are asked to write an article, you should be clear about its purpose, audience and topic. Understanding the purpose, audience and topic will help you to judge the formality required for your writing. For example, if you are asked to write an article specifically for teenagers, the information you include and the tone you use will be adapted for them – although you need to remember that a certain degree of formality (such as avoiding slang, text speak and colloquial language) and correct punctuation will still be essential.

Articles can be written about virtually anything, from topics such as fashion and film to the environment and local events. Some articles are lively and light-hearted and you may be able to use a range of humour. Other articles can be relatively serious and you may have to voice your concerns over a given topic or event.

Activity 1

Look at the table below. You will see a number of statements about articles. Read these carefully and decide whether the information is true or false.

Statement	True or false?
You must include a title for your article.	
Pictures are important and you will lose marks if you do not include them.	
Articles will begin with an introduction so the topic is clear.	
You can use a range of persuasive techniques, where relevant.	
You can use topic sentences to introduce each new idea within a paragraph.	
Paragraphs are not important in an article.	
Articles need a conclusion.	
Articles are always very short pieces of opinion writing.	
Articles are only found in newspapers.	

Activity 2

It is important that you understand exactly what you are being asked to write when you produce an article. You also need to think carefully about the target audience and using an appropriate tone. There are two exam-style tasks below. The first one has been annotated for you. Read the first exam-style task and the annotations carefully and then read the second task, adding your own annotations.

Exam-style task 1

> You have been asked to produce a lively article for a magazine persuading others about the benefits of exercise. **[20]**

'Lively' suggests it will be full of life and characterized by excitement and energy.

This tells you exactly what you are being asked to write.

This is such a general topic. You can write about exercise in general or could choose a specific aspect or type.

The purpose of the article is to inform the readers about exercise and then to persuade (to either do more, less, be healthy, etc.).

'Benefits' suggests the advantages and gains you get from doing something. It is possible to write an article suggesting there are no benefits (although this might be difficult to sustain given that exercise is proven to be beneficial).

Exam-style task 2

> The area where you live has recently been voted as untidy and neglected by local residents. You have been asked to produce an article for a local newspaper about a campaign to tidy up the area where you live. **[20]**

Tip

Titles

Writing a headline for a magazine or newspaper article can be a time-consuming task. Some professional writers can spend days tweaking their title and coming up with something eye-catching and effective. You have very little time in the exam to devote to thinking about a title. It is a good idea to write the article first and hopefully a title will come to you as you are writing. There are a number of different techniques for titles but the following are essential, so make sure your title:

- links to the content
- catches the reader's interest.

Activity

Read the titles below and see if you can match at least one technique (some titles use more than one technique) to each title.

Twist of fete as tornado hits school fun day

Celebrity Big Blubber   **Flu York City**

Grand theft of morality – should we stand up to new PS3 game?

Grab a pizza the action!

DEVASTATING FLOOD FLATTENS WHOLE CITY

Caught short? Don't get caught out: pay your tax by direct debit

Pun (play on words)

Direct appeal

Questions

Shock tactic

Alliteration

You can include a range of persuasive and effective techniques in an article to engage your reader, but you must make sure that techniques are not included at the expense of the fluency of the rest of your work.

Activity

The student article opposite is ambitious. They have some great ideas and use a range of techniques as well as a lively tone. Read the article carefully and then answer the questions below.

1. Read the article again and highlight all of the different techniques used by the student. Make a note of each different technique. The first one has been done for you.

2. Can you spot any errors in sentence construction and punctuation?

3. The real problem with this article is that the student is so fixed on writing in a lively style that they jump from one idea to the next without developing or making each idea clear. Choose one paragraph from the article and see if you can rewrite it, adding more detail and making the information sound less disjointed.

The Joys of Exercise

Imagine. You're drenched in sweat, gasping for breath and your legs are so tired you think they are going to fall off. Appealing? I consider the gym to be more of a social meeting place for my friends and me. Well, why not? My cute Nike crop tops look dashing with some pink trainers and shorts. After all, the sportmax look is so in this season! I mean, who would really want to sweat up a new t-shirt anyway?

You hear women completely excited by the prospect of losing 300 calories on the treadmill. You know the truth, love — within one minute of leaving the gym the aromatic smells of the Chinese takeaway will make you surrender. Hey, who cares? It's relatively low fat anyway.

Back to exercise. What sport would you choose? Football? Hell, no. Lycra is so unflattering, and only in your dreams will you look like Keira Knightley from *Bend It Like Beckham*. But you know what is exciting? Watching football. A 90-minute match is so exciting it will seem like a 30-minute workout anyway! Right then, if football is a no, what next? Rugby? No! If you want butch thighs, a broken nose and to be half-strangled in a scrum be my guest, but all that mud totally ruins a manicure! Hockey? No. Enough said. In fact, I wouldn't recommend any ball sports.

Swimming leads to frazzled hair from the yucky chlorine, and the changing rooms are always dirty anyway. You have to strip off in front of total strangers (or, worse still, your friends) and have you seen what they wear? Well, not much, is it? Who would really want to be humiliated by some totally gorgeous, stick thin zombies who see you munching on a bacon buttie (from the chip shop opposite the pool) only to say: 'Wow, you're so brave. That looks so nice but my figure is so important to me.' Ouch.

Imperative verb – direct command to reader

Activity 5

Read the following exam-style task:

> Write an article for your school magazine about the importance of saving energy. Give suggestions to your fellow students on how to be more environmentally friendly. **[20]**

Now look at the plan below and complete it with your own ideas in response to the exam-style task.

Area of article	Your notes
Effective title – linked to the environment	
Introduction – general importance of saving energy – why the article is being written	
Paragraph 1 – how to be environmentally friendly at school	
Paragraph 2 – how to be environmentally friendly at home	
Paragraph 3 – how to be environmentally friendly generally (community, socially, etc.)	
Conclusion – overall suggestions	

Activity 6

One student completed their article and their teacher gave them the following feedback:

> This is well written and clear but I'd like you to read back through and see where this can be improved.

1. Read through the article opposite. What do you think of the article?
2. Is there sufficient detail?
3. Would this article encourage you to save energy? Why (or why not)?
4. Make a list of five things that the student could add or adjust to improve their work.

Energy Saving

Look around you. Can you see the lights switched on when it is light outside? Is the radiator on, yet the windows are open? Is the TV on standby or your computer on but not being used? If you answered yes to any of these, then you are wasting energy.

Energy costs money. FACT. But not only are you wasting hard-earned money, you are also putting the environment at risk. Leaving the light on in an empty room is an eco no-no. Think of the polar bears in the Antarctic. The more energy you use, the more CO_2 is released. This is a greenhouse gas and contributes to global warming which melts the ice in the Antarctic. Every day a polar bear or its family loses its home and many die as a result of global warming.

On average, this school wastes around £800 a year on excess energy. Think of what the school could do with that money! More equipment, better food and perhaps those locks on the toilets might get repaired! So, if you see an eco no-no occurring, sort it out.

If you are the last to leave the room, turn that light out. If possible, don't even turn it on, open the blinds instead. If it is a cold day, don't turn on the heating, put on a jumper or even a lab coat. If you find the heating is on, ask the teacher if it's OK to turn it down as you're too hot. Close open windows if they are not necessary but please make sure your teacher is happy for you to do so. We don't want any detentions now, do we? After your IT lesson, shut down your computer, especially if it's the last lesson of the day.

If you do just one of these suggestions every day, as well as your own, you'll be well on the way to becoming an eco-warrior. Try them out at home and you'll earn endless brownie points from the money you save your parents. Maybe a raise in pocket money would be in order...

Activity 7

You have been asked to write your own article about the importance of saving energy. Use the plan you made in Activity 5 and your suggestions for improving the student sample article in Activity 6. Remember to use the following checklist to help you with your work:

- Include an effective title (this can be added at the end).

- Structure your work in clear paragraphs, using topic sentences and developing your details.

- Use a range of techniques to appeal to your reader.

- Try to make your writing interesting and appealing (so you don't bore the reader).

- Include an effective conclusion.

7 Leaflets

Assessment Objectives

- **AO5**
  – 1 Communicate clearly, effectively and imaginatively, selecting and adapting tone, style and register for different forms, purposes and audiences.
  – 2 Organize information and ideas, using structural and grammatical features to support coherence and cohesion of texts.

- **AO6**
  – Candidates must use a range of vocabulary and sentence structures for clarity, purpose and effect, with accurate spelling and punctuation.

One of the types of tasks you may face in your Component 2 Writing exam could ask you to write a leaflet. Leaflets are commonly used to give information and advice or to persuade someone to take action. For example, a leaflet advertising a tourist attraction is written to give information about the attraction and to persuade the reader to visit. A health leaflet found in a hospital or health clinic is written to give information about a medical condition, to help people who may be suffering or to give advice on how to cope with a specific illness or issue. Leaflets can vary hugely depending on their format, and visual features of the leaflet will be adapted depending on the content.

The purpose of the leaflet (inform, advise, persuade) will often determine the features, the content and the presentation. For example, a leaflet offering help to families suffering a loss or bereavement may use muted colours and will contain calm, reassuring language. A leaflet advertising a theme park will often be vividly coloured with an explosion of action-filled pictures and plenty of dynamic language, including lively verbs. If you are asked to produce a leaflet in the exam, it is essential that you carefully consider the topic you are being asked to write about, the given audience and the features that you will use.

Activity 1

1. Below is a plan for the features of a leaflet. The labels around it give more information about the purpose of each feature. Copy out the diagram and draw an arrow to match each label to the correct feature of the leaflet.

2. Can you think of any other persuasive features or techniques that may help when writing a leaflet? Make a list of any that you can think of.

Tip

Top tips for writing leaflets:

- Slogans are a good idea: make them short and snappy and only ever use one exclamation mark, if it is a necessary piece of punctuation to add.

- Use personal pronouns (I, we, he, she, etc.) to personalize the information to the reader.

- Keep your work neat so that you have an immediate visual impact on the reader.

- Keep it clear and informative (don't wander off topic or over-write).

Pictures can inform the reader or make them empathize. Write down what the picture will show – do not waste time drawing it.

Use subheadings, where necessary, to introduce new ideas or topics.

- xxx
- xxx
- xxx
- xxx

Picture of....

Picture of....

Address:

Telephone:

Website:

A heading should make it clear what the leaflet is about.

Contact details are a common feature of leaflets.

You may choose to include a bullet point section of facts but the rest of the leaflet must be written in sentences.

Activity ②

Look at the following exam-style task:

You have been asked to write a leaflet for local Year 6 students giving information about your school. You have been told to comment on the following areas:

- the teachers
- the subjects studied
- the facilities

- sporting activities
- clubs
- any other useful information. **[20]**

1. Spend five minutes making a list of the key information about each of these areas that would be useful for a prospective new student. Use the table below to help you record your ideas.

Teachers	Subjects studied	Facilities	Sporting activities	Clubs	Other information

2. Now, using a piece of paper, spend five minutes sketching out a plan as to how you might structure your leaflet.

Remember: you are assessed on the written content of your work, so do not spend too much time on the visual aspect of the task.

Activity ③

A student has written the following paragraph in their leaflet.

Although we get good exam results, our school is really boring. We are in the middle of the countryside so you will have to get a bus here which is a pain in the morning. My bus journey is excruciating as I am one of the first to board and am bored to tears by the time I reach school. Another negative point about our school is the uniform. Not only do we look like frogs in our green blazers but the purple tie makes us appear like characters out of Harry Potter rather than a dull little local country school. The blazers are expensive and the fabric is durable and hard wearing but this makes them extremely hot which causes extreme overheating.

Read the task in Activity 2 again. Make a list of anything the student has done above which doesn't quite follow what they have been asked to do.

Activity 4

Read the leaflet below. This student was asked to produce a leaflet about smoking. Look carefully at the teacher's comment for this piece of work and then select one of the paragraphs from the leaflet. Using any additional information or research, develop the paragraph trying to make it more effective and interesting while retaining an impact on the reader.

Smoking KILLS!

So you smoke? Why? Maybe because:

- You think it's cool.
- Your friends do it.
- You feel it relieves stress.

Or maybe it's because you want to die young? FACT: Every cigarette you smoke takes 5 minutes off your life. If you smoked 12 a day, that's an hour off your life every day. If you did this every day for a year, that's 365 hours off your life. Most people smoke more than this.

Maybe it's because you want cancer? FACT: 60% of all smokers end up with some sort of cancer or serious organ failure later in life. That could be heart problems, liver problems, kidney problems or a series of other equally life-threatening things.

Maybe it's because you want to be unattractive? FACT: As you smoke, you are damaging your hair, teeth, nails, skin, and even your eyes become bloodshot.

Maybe you don't want to find a partner? FACT: cigarettes cause seriously bad breath and make you smell awful. Nobody is going to want to kiss someone like that.

Maybe you actually want to fill your body with poison? FACT: Almost every ingredient used to make a cigarette is poison. The three main chemicals are lethal and you are putting them into your body.

Have I guessed correctly yet? No? Well, how about this? Maybe it's because you want to kill those around you? FACT: One in three people who die from smoking each year have never actually smoked a cigarette.

So go on, tell me why do YOU smoke? If you want to know more or need help quitting, visit our website at www.help2quit.com or phone our free helpline on 01112 762897.

Remember, your decision could be affecting other people's lives.

Teacher's comment

You have included a wealth of persuasive features in your writing and appeal to the reader. Some of your ideas, while effective, lack any real detail or development. Some sentences contain lists of effects but there is no sense of the real impact of these due to a lack of detail.

Assessment Criteria for Writing: Component 2, Section B

	AO5 Communication and organization *12 marks*	AO6 Vocabulary, sentence structure, spelling and punctuation *8 marks*
Band 5	**11–12 marks** • Shows sophisticated understanding of the purpose and format of the task. • Shows sustained awareness of the reader/intended audience. • Appropriate register is confidently adapted to purpose/audience. • Content is ambitious, pertinent and sophisticated. • Ideas are convincingly developed and supported by a range of relevant details. • There is sophistication in the shape and structure of the writing. • Communication has ambition and sophistication.	**8 marks** • There is appropriate and effective variation of sentence structures. • Virtually all sentence construction is controlled and accurate. • A range of punctuation is used confidently and accurately. • Virtually all spelling, including that of complex irregular words, is correct. • Control of tense and agreement is totally secure. • A wide range of appropriate, ambitious vocabulary is used to create effect or convey precise meaning.
Band 4	**8–10 marks** • Shows consistent understanding of the purpose and format of the task. • Shows secure awareness of the reader/intended audience. • Register is appropriately and consistently adapted to purpose/audience. • Content is well judged and detailed. • Ideas are organized and coherently developed with supporting detail. • There is clear shape and structure in the writing (paragraphs are used effectively to give sequence and organization). • Communication has clarity, fluency and some ambition.	**6–7 marks** • Sentence structure is varied to achieve particular effects. • Control of sentence construction is secure. • A range of punctuation is used accurately. • Spelling, including that of irregular words, is secure. • Control of tense and agreement is secure. • Vocabulary is ambitious and used with precision.

	AO5 Communication and organization *12 marks*	AO6 Vocabulary, sentence structure, spelling and punctuation *8 marks*
Band 3	**5–7 marks** • Shows clear understanding of the purpose and format of the task. • Shows clear awareness of the reader/intended audience. • Register is appropriately adapted to purpose/audience. • Content is developed and appropriate reasons are given in support of opinions/ideas. • Ideas are organized into coherent arguments. • There is some shape and structure in the writing (paragraphs are used to give sequence and organization). • Communication has clarity and fluency.	**4–5 marks** • There is variety in sentence structure. • Control of sentence construction is mostly secure. • A range of punctuation is used, mostly accurately. • Most spelling, including that of irregular words, is correct. • Control of tense and agreement is mostly secure. • Vocabulary is beginning to develop and is used with some precision.
Band 2	**3–4 marks** • Shows awareness of the reader/intended audience. • A clear attempt to adapt register to purpose/audience. • Some reasons are given in support of opinions and ideas. • Limited development of ideas. • Some sequencing of ideas into paragraphs (structure/direction may be uncertain). • Communication has some clarity and fluency.	**2–3 marks** • Some variety of sentence structure. • There is some control of sentence construction. • Some control of a range of punctuation. • Spelling is usually accurate. • Control of tense and agreement is generally secure. • There is some range of vocabulary.
Band 1	**1–2 marks** • Basic awareness of the purpose and format of the task. • Some basic awareness of the reader/intended audience. • Some attempt to adapt register to purpose/audience (e.g. degree of formality). • Some relevant content despite uneven coverage of the topic. • Content may be thin and brief. • Simple sequencing of ideas (paragraphs may be used to show obvious divisions or group ideas into some order). • There is some basic clarity but communication of meaning is limited.	**1 mark** • Limited range of sentence structure. • Control of sentence construction is limited. • There is some attempt to use punctuation. • Some spelling is accurate. • Control of tense and agreement is limited. • Limited range of vocabulary.
	0 marks • Nothing worthy of credit.	**0 marks** • Nothing worthy of credit.

Sample exam papers

In this chapter, you will have the opportunity to complete a sample exam paper for both Component 1 and Component 2.

The exam at a glance

	Component 1	Component 2
Reading: Section A	**20th-century literature reading** • 40 marks • 10 minutes reading • 50 minutes answering	**19th and 21st-century non-fiction reading** • 40 marks • 10 minutes reading • 50 minutes answering
Writing: Section B	**Creative prose writing** • 40 marks • Choose one task from a choice of four. • 10 minutes planning • 35 minutes writing	**Transactional/persuasive writing** • 40 marks • Complete two compulsory tasks. • 30 minutes on each question (5 minutes planning and 25 minutes writing)

What do I need to do in the exam?

Read the information on the front cover of the exam paper very carefully. These guidelines have been written to help you. An example of guidelines from the Component 1 exam are included below.

The instructions to candidates on the front of the exam papers contain advice about how to spend your time. For Component 1, it is suggested that you spend approximately 10 minutes reading and 50 minutes answering the reading questions, 10 minutes planning your response to your chosen writing task and 35 minutes writing your narrative account. These times are guidelines only. You may decide to spend five minutes planning and reserve five minutes for proofreading your work, for example.

INSTRUCTIONS TO CANDIDATES

Use black ink or black ball-point pen.

Answer all questions in Section A.

Select one title to use for your writing in Section B.

Write your answers in the separate answer book provided.

You are advised to spend your time as follows:

Section A   – about 10 minutes reading
            – about 50 minutes answering the questions

Section B   – about 10 minutes planning
            – about 35 minutes writing

You have 1 hour and 45 minutes to complete the paper.

The number of marks is given in brackets at the end of each question or part-question.

Component 1 and Component 2: Reading

In an English Reading exam, it is always sensible to be methodical and thoughtful. The following advice might help you:

- Always read the advice before the first question. This information may give you some background to the texts. Sometimes the information before a question can direct you to look at a specific section of the text.

- Keep an eye on the time. Your teacher will have suggested how long you should spend on each question and you should follow their advice.

- Always check how many marks a question is worth, as this will give you some indication as to how long you should spend on your answer.

- Read each question carefully. Then read the question again. You may need to annotate the question to ensure you fully understand what you are being asked to do.

- When reading through a specified section of text, it can be helpful to use a highlighter to pick out key evidence.

- Always approach a source text in chronological order, so you are able to track through the text. If you answer in a chronological way, it will make your work seem both thoughtful and measured.

Component 1: Writing

You will have a choice of four creative prose writing tasks in the Component 1 Writing exam. You should only choose **one** of these.

- Try to choose the title that most appeals to you and that you think you can write about.

- After you have chosen your title, spend a few minutes planning your work. Think about a clear beginning, middle and end for your narrative. You may wish to use a spider diagram or a flow chart to think about the sequence of events, the characters and the setting.

- Keep an eye on the time. You do not want to run out of time and risk leaving your narrative incomplete.

- When you have finished your narrative, proofread your work. Check your work one sentence at a time as this will help you to check whether your writing makes sense.

Component 2: Writing

In the Writing section of the Component 2 exam, you will have to complete **two** writing tasks.

- Try to work out the purpose of the writing tasks. Are you being asked to persuade or inform, for example?

- Consider who you are being asked to write to for each task. This will help you to judge the tone and formality of your writing.

- Spend a few minutes planning your work. Think about the information you would like to include and how you will sequence this.

- Plan your time carefully to ensure that you have enough time to complete both tasks.

- Proofread your responses at the end of the exam.

Component 1

Section A Reading: 40 marks

Read carefully the passage below. Then answer all the questions which follow it.

Beyond the window of my father's shop, midwinter light skims the snow. My father stands, straightening his back.

'How was school?' he asks.

'Good,' I say.

5   He puts his sander down and reaches for his jacket on a hook. […]

My father and I leave his workshop in the barn and walk out into the cold. The air, dry and still, hurts my nose as I breathe. We lace up our snowshoes and bang them hard against the crust. A rust colour is on the bark, and the sun is making purple shadows behind the trees. From time to time the light sends up a sheen of pocked glass.

10   We move at a good clip, dodging pine boughs, occasionally catching a shower on the back of the neck. My father says, 'I feel like a dog let out to exercise at the end of the day.'

The stillness of the forest is always a surprise, as if an audience had quieted for a performance. Beneath the hush I can hear the rustle of dead leaves, the snap of a twig, a brook running under a skin of ice. […] We follow a path that is familiar, that will end at a stone wall near the summit. The wall, square on three sides, once
15   bordered a farmer's property. When we reach the wall, my father will sometimes sit on it and have a cigarette.

[…] Taking a hike together is a habit my father and I have grown into. My father spends too many hours bent to his work, and I know he needs to get outside. […]

A branch snaps and scratches my cheek. The sun sets. We have maybe twenty minutes left of decent light. The route back to the house is easy all the way down and can be done in less than ten. We still have time to
20   reach the wall.

I hear the first cry then, and I think it is a cat. I stop under a canopy of pine and listen, and there it is again. A rhythmic cry, a wail.

'Dad,' I say.

I take a step toward the sound, but as abruptly as it began, it ends. Behind me snow falls with a muted
25   thump onto the crust.

'A cat,' my father says.

We begin the steep climb up the hill. My feet feel heavy at the ends of my legs. When we reach the summit, my father will judge the light, and if there's time he'll sit on the stone wall and see if he can make out our house – a smidgen of yellow through the trees. '*There*,' he will say to me, pointing down the hill, 'can you see
30   it now?'

[…] I follow his tracks and pride myself that I no longer have any trouble keeping up with him. Over his shoulder he tosses me a Werther's candy, and I catch it on the fly. I pull off my mittens, tuck them under my arm, and begin to unwrap the cellophane. As I do I hear the distant thunk of a car door shutting.

35 We listen to the sound of an engine revving. It seems to come from the direction of a motel on the northeast side of the hill. […]

I hear a third cry then – heartbreaking, beseeching, winding down to shuddering. […]

In his snowshoes he begins to run as best he can in the direction of the cry. Every dozen steps he stops, letting the sound guide him. I follow, and the sky darkens as we go. He takes a flashlight from his pocket and switches it on.

40 'Dad,' I say, panic rising in my chest.

The beam of light jiggles on the snow as he runs. My father begins to sweep the flashlight in an arc, back and forth, side to side. The moon lifts off the horizon, a companion in our search. […]

We move laterally around the base of the slope. The flashlight flickers off and my father shakes it to reconnect the batteries. It slips out of his glove and falls into a soft pocket of snow beside a tree, making an
45 eerie cone of light beneath the crust. He bends to pick it up, and as he raises himself, the light catches on a patch of blue plaid through the trees.

'Hello!' he calls.

The woods are silent, mocking him, as if this were a game.

My father waves the flashlight back and forth. I'm wondering if we shouldn't turn around and head back to
50 the house. It's dangerous in the woods at night; it's too easy to get lost. My father makes another pass with the flashlight, and then another, and it seems he has to make twenty passes before he catches again the patch of blue plaid.

There's a sleeping bag in the snow, a corner of flannel turned over at its opening.

'Stay here,' my father says.

55 I watch my father run forward in his snowshoes, the way one sometimes does in dreams – unable to make the legs move fast enough. […] When he reaches the plaid flannel, he tears it open. I hear him make a sound unlike any I have ever heard before. He falls to his knees in the snow.

'Dad!' I shout, already running toward him.

My arms are flailing, and it feels as though someone is pushing against my chest. My hat falls off, but I keep
60 on clumping through the snow. I am breathing hard when I reach him, and he doesn't tell me to go away. I look down at the sleeping bag.

A small face gazes up at me, the eyes wide despite their many folds. […] The baby is wrapped in a bloody towel, and its lips are blue.

My father bends his cheek to the tiny mouth. […] With one swift movement he gathers up the icy sleeping
65 bag, presses it close to him, and stands.

[…] He sets his bundle down, unzips his jacket, and tears open his flannel shirt, the buttons popping as he goes. He unwraps the infant from the bloody towel. […] My father puts the child close to his skin, holding the head upright in the palm of one hand. Without even knowing that I've looked, I understand the infant is a girl.

My father staggers to his feet. He wraps his flannel shirt and parka around the child, folding the jacket tight
70 with his arms. […]

'Nicky,' my father says.

I look up at him.

'Hold on to my jacket if you need to,' he says, 'but don't let yourself get more than a foot or two behind me.'

I grab the edge of his parka. […]

75 We move by the smell of smoke. Sometimes we have the scent, and sometimes we don't. I can see the silhouettes of trees, but not their branches.

'Hang in there,' my father says, but I don't know if it is to me or to the infant against his chest that he is speaking.

We half slide, half run down the long hill, my thighs burning with the strain. My father lost the flashlight when
80 he left the sleeping bag in the snow, and there isn't time to go back for it. We move through the trees, and the boughs scratch my face. My hair and neck are soaked from melted snow that freezes again on my forehead. From time to time I feel a rising fear: We are lost, and we won't get the baby out in time. She will die in my father's arms. No, no, I tell myself, we won't let that happen. If we miss the house, we'll eventually hit the highway. We have to.

85 I see the light from a lamp in my father's workshop. […]

The last hundred yards seems the longest distance I have ever run in my life. […] My father sits in a chair. He opens his jacket and looks down at the tiny face. The baby's eyes are closed, the lips still bluish. He puts the back of his hand to the mouth, and from the way he closes his eyes I can tell that she's breathing.

(from *Light on Snow* by Anita Shreve)

Read lines 1–17.

A1 What impression do you get of the relationship between the father and daughter? **[10]**

Read lines 18–35.

A2 How does the writer show that the story is set in a rural location? **[5]**

Read lines 36–57.

A3 How does the writer make these lines tense and dramatic? **[10]**

Read lines 58–68.

A4 Make a list of details about the baby in the 'sleeping bag'. **[5]**

Read lines 69–88.

A5 How do you react to what happens in these lines? Are they an effective ending to the passage? **[10]**

Component 1

Section B Writing: 40 marks

In this section you will be assessed for the quality of your creative prose writing skills.

24 marks are awarded for communication and organization; 16 marks are awarded for vocabulary, sentence structure, spelling and punctuation.

You should aim to write about 450–600 words.

Choose **one** of the following titles for your writing: **[40]**

Either,	(a)	It was a tough decision.
Or,	(b)	The Visitor.
Or,	(c)	Write about a time when you did something embarrassing.
Or,	(d)	Write a story which begins: 'I didn't know what to do for the best…'

Component 2

Section A Reading: 40 marks

*Answer **all** the following questions.*

The Resource Material for use with Section A is a newspaper article, 'The cotton in your clothes may be made by girls aged 11, paid £6 a month', by Robin Pagnamenta on pages 172–173.

The extract on page 174 is from a book by Friedrich Engels, The Condition of the Working Class in England, written in 1844.

Read the newspaper article by Robin Pagnamenta on pages 172–173.

A1 (a) How many cotton mills are there in India?   **[1]**

(b) Approximately how many girls are employed in Tamil Nadu?   **[1]**

(c) How much of the global trade for cotton does India export?   **[1]**

A2 Robin Pagnamenta is trying to persuade us that the teenage girls employed in Indian cotton mills have a difficult life. How does he try to do this?   **[10]**

You should comment on:
- what he says to influence readers
- his use of language and tone
- the way he presents his argument.

To answer the following questions you will need to read the extract on page 174 by Friedrich Engels.

A3 (a) What does the writer mean by 'it is like living in the midst of an army just returned from a campaign' in lines 30–31?   **[1]**

(b) What does the writer suggest can happen to a girl's body if they work in the 'throstle room'? **[2]**

A4 What do you think and feel about Friedrich Engels's views about mill work? **[10]**

You should comment on:
- what is said
- how it is said.

You must refer to the text to support your comments.

To answer the following questions you will need to use both texts.

A5 According to these two writers, why should consumers change their attitudes to the people who produce their clothes? **[4]**

A6 Both of these texts are about child labour. Compare the following:

- the writers' attitudes to the treatment of girls who work in clothing mills
- how they get across their arguments. **[10]**

You must use the text to support your comments and make it clear which text you get your information from.

The cotton in your clothes may be made by girls aged 11, paid £6 a month

Girls as young as 11 are being paid as little as £6 a month to produce the raw materials used to make garments for sale in Britain, an investigation by *The Times* has found. Girls are sold to cotton spinning
5 mills in the southern state of Tamil Nadu, locked in for weeks on end and forced to work relentless hours for pitiful wages in dangerous conditions.

'It's a prison life,' says Saraswati, 21, from Kadamalaikundu village in a hill district in India's
10 deep south. After ten months working 12-hour shifts, six days a week, at the Amarjothi Spinning Mill, she was desperate and suffering nosebleeds from inhaling cotton dust. 'I kept saying I want to go home, but they refused,' she said. 'In the end, I
15 contacted my brother and told him, "If you don't take me away, I'm going to kill myself". He came and fought with the management and took me away.'

The yarn produced from raw cotton fibre by
20 India's 1,943 mills is a key material used to make garments for western brands at other factories in the country and overseas, including Bangladesh and China. Buyers of finished garments from southern Indian factories include several big names on

the British high streets. Industry experts say it is 25 almost impossible, despite the efforts of retailers, to have complete ethical oversight on the entire supply chain of cotton – from farm, to yarn mill, to garment manufacturer, to shop.

Like thousands of other teenage girls from 30 the impoverished Theni district of Tamil Nadu, Saraswati and her parents were persuaded by a broker to sign her up for a three-year contract known as a 'Sumangali' scheme. Under the terms, she would live in a factory dormitory and be paid 35 1,500 rupees (£15) a month, with a lump sum of 40,000 rupees at the end of the contract – if she completed it. Many do not. In Tamil, the word Sumangali means 'a long, healthy life with a husband'. The suggestion is that the lump sum can 40 be used for a dowry to secure a good husband. In reality, this system of bonded labour – under which an estimated 200,000 girls are employed at many of the 1,600 spinning mills across Tamil Nadu, where the industry is focused – amounts to a form 45 of slavery. 'Some girls jumped over the walls to escape,' said Selvarani, 21, who worked at another mill in Coimbatore for three years. 'There was no other way to leave. There were guards to make sure we couldn't get out.' Selvarani, who suffered a permanent knee injury after being forced to stand without rest during months of gruelling night shifts operating machinery, said one colleague died while jumping over the wall. Local activists say they are aware of 89 suicides and unexplained deaths in spinning mills in the state over the past five years. They believe the true figure is higher.

At one mill *The Times* visited in Tiruppur last week, the incessant clatter of machinery, extreme heat, humidity and cotton dust made for brutal conditions. Spindles and other machinery must be kept running 24 hours a day, operated round the clock by teenage girls overseen by male supervisors. 'I would start at 8am and finish at 9.30pm,' said Mayilaayee, 17, from Tangamallapuram village. 'I had to stand up all the time. The supervisors would shout at us if we sat down.'

A financial incentive exists for mills to lose workers before the end of their terms, prompting many to make conditions so intolerable that employees – who are not allowed phones and can go out only once a month accompanied by guards – quit voluntarily. Brokers, who source girls from poor families in rural areas, often targeting those hit by bad harvests, are typically paid 1,000 to 5,000 rupees a girl by the mills on arrival. A second commission is paid if girls stay longer than six months, when they are given permission for their first home visit. Ramiya, 18, from the village of Paloothu, said that when she joined a Sumangali scheme at Rajave Textiles in Sulur, she was paid 600 rupees a month. She never received a promised lump sum of 35,000 rupees because she quit after ten months. Raja Lakshmi, 17, says she was taken to work in a mill in Coimbatore by her parents when she was 11 years old. 'I wasn't able to do the work so they let me go,' she said.

India is the world's biggest exporter of cotton yarn, with £3.5 billion of the £12.7 billion global trade. The state of Tamil Nadu contributes 60 per cent of national production and is home to the bulk of India's mills, which employ 400,000 people.

In the spinning heartland of Vedasandur, 186 giant mills are sprawled across a bucolic landscape near the ancient Hindu temple town of Madurai. Surrounded by high walls, topped with barbed wire and metal gates patrolled by guards, from the outside they look more like prisons than factories. Although most western brands police conditions in the factories where their finished garments are cut and stitched, only a handful try to map their supply chains and audit factories where their yarn is spun. These include Primark, Mothercare and C&A, which have formed a working group under the Ethical Trade Initiative (ETI) to do so.

Marijn Peepercamp, of the India Committee of the Netherlands, which published a report on the abuses recently called Flawed Fabrics, said the vast majority of buyers 'do not engage in monitoring and corrective actions at the level of the spinning mills'. 'These are gross human violations on a huge scale,' she said. 'Consumers should ask where their clothes are made, but it's also up to governments like the UK to hold brands accountable.'

The Condition of the Working Class in England
by Friedrich Engels

But besides all this, there are some branches of factory work which have an especially injurious effect. In many rooms of the cotton and flax-spinning mills, the air is filled with fibrous dust, which produces chest affections especially among workers in the carding and combing-rooms. Some constitutions can bear it, some cannot; but the operative has no choice. He must take the room in which he finds

5 work, whether his chest is sound or not. The most common effects of this breathing of dust are blood-spitting, hard, and noisy breathing, pains in the chest, coughs, sleeplessness – in short, all the symptoms of asthma ending in the worst cases in consumption. Especially unwholesome is the wet spinning of linen-yarn which is carried on by young boys and girls. The water spurts over them from the spindle, so that the front of their clothing is constantly wet through to the skin; and there is always

10 water standing on the floor. This is the case to a less degree in the doubling-rooms of the cotton mills, and the result is a constant succession of cold and affections of the chest. A hoarse, rough voice is common to all operatives, but especially to wet spinners and doublers.

Stuart, Mackintosh, and Sir D. Barry express themselves in the most vigorous terms as to the unwholesomeness of this work, and the small consideration shown by most of the manufacturers for

15 the health of the girls who do it. Another effect of flax-spinning is a peculiar deformity of the shoulder, especially a projection of the right shoulder-blade, consequent upon the nature of the work. This sort of spinning and the throstle-spinning of cotton frequently produce diseases of the kneepan, which is used to check the spindle during the joining of broken threads. The frequent stooping and the bending to the low machine common to both these branches of work have, in general, a stunting effect upon

20 the growth of the operative. In the throstle-room of the cotton mill at Manchester, in which I was employed, I do not remember to have seen one single tall, well-built girl; they were all short, dumpy, and badly formed, decidedly ugly in the whole development of the figure. But apart from all these diseases and malformations, the limbs of the operatives suffer in still another way. The work between the machinery gives rise to a multitude of accidents of more or less serious nature, which have for

25 the operative the secondary effect of unfitting him for his work more or less completely. The most common accident is the squeezing off of a single joint of a finger, somewhat less common the loss of the whole finger, half or a whole hand, and arm, etc., in the machinery. Lockjaw very often follows, even upon the lesser among these injuries, and brings death with it.

Besides the deformed persons, a great number of maimed ones may be seen going about in

30 Manchester; this one has lost an arm or a part of one, that one a foot, the third half a leg; it is like living in the midst of an army just returned from a campaign. But the most dangerous portion of the machinery is the strapping which conveys a motive power from the shaft to the separate machines, especially if it contains buckles, which, however, are rarely used now. Whoever is seized by the strapping is carried out with lightning speed, thrown against the ceiling above and floor below with

35 such force that there is rarely a whole bone left in the body, and death follows instantly.

Component 2

Section B Writing: 40 marks

Answer Question B1 and Question B2.

In this section you will be assessed for the quality of your writing skills.

For each question, 12 marks are awarded for communication and organization; 8 marks are

awarded for vocabulary, sentence structure, punctuation and spelling.

Think about the purpose and audience for your writing.

You should aim to write about 300–400 words for each task.

B1 Your school/college has asked students to produce an article about their experience of working/part time jobs.

Write an article about your experience of work.

You could include:
- your thoughts and feelings about the work experience
- your experience of paid work.   **[20]**

B2 A proposal has been made to hold a charity sporting event in the grounds of your school and the surrounding local area.

You have decided to write a letter to your community magazine to share your views on this proposal. You could write in favour of or against this proposal.

Write a lively letter to the magazine giving your views.   **[20]**

Analyse: to examine something methodically and in detail, in order to explain and interpret it

Analysis: detailed examination of something

Anti-climax: a disappointing ending to a series of events that seemed to be leading to a point of great interest or excitement

Call to action: an instruction often found at the end of an advert, leaflet or charity letter such as 'Don't delay!'

Chronologically: arranged in the order in which things occurred

Clearly: a point made that is easy to understand

Convincing: to make someone feel certain that something is true

Detail(s): individual fact(s) or feature(s)

Dialogue: the words spoken by characters in a play, film or story

Effectively: a point made that achieves what you want it to do – it has an effect

Evaluate: to form an idea of; to assess and decide a value

Evidence: a fact or piece of information that gives a reason for believing something

Explicit: openly/exactly stated or expressed

Implicit: meaning that is suggested but not directly expressed

Interpret: to explain the meaning of something said or written, or of someone's actions

Judgement: a considered decision or sensible conclusion

Location: the exact place of something

Question: a sentence that asks for information or an answer

Range: a wide selection of different relevant points

Scan: to glance through a text to find a key word or piece of information

Synthesize: to combine or put together

Topic sentence: the key sentence that explains what a paragraph is about